P9-BYS-488

TOUCHPOINTS FOR TROUBLED TIMES
God's Answers for Your Daily Needs

Other TouchPoints Products:

TouchPoints for Couples
TouchPoints for Men
TouchPoints for Students
TouchPoints for Women
TouchPoints Bible Promises
The TouchPoint Bible

TouchPoints
for Troubled Times

GOD'S ANSWERS FOR
YOUR DAILY NEEDS

Tyndale House Publishers, Inc.
Wheaton, Illinois

Visit Tyndale's exciting Web site at www.tyndale.com

General editors: Ronald A. Beers and V. Gilbert Beers

Managing editor: Linda Taylor

Contributing writers: V. Gilbert Beers, Ronald A. Beers, Brian R. Coffey,
Jonathan D. Gray, Shawn A. Harrison, Sanford D. Hull, Rhonda K.
O'Brien, Douglas J. Rumford, Linda Taylor

Designed by Beth Sparkman

Edited by Linda Taylor

ISBN 0-8423-8728-5

Printed in the United States of America

09 08 07 06 05 04
8   7   6   5   4   3

PREFACE

Psalm 46:1 *God is our refuge and strength, always ready to help in times of trouble.*

Few would characterize our days today as free of trouble. As we consider the tension in our world, we often cannot help but feel a tinge of fear. We look to the heavens and ask, "God, what are you up to?" We may even momentarily wonder if the God we look to as sovereign Creator hasn't, for a time, lost control.

It is just at those times that we must listen to his answer—the answer he gives us in the pages of his Word. What he is "up to" is no different from what he has been "up to" since time began. He continues to write the story of salvation in the lives of people all over the globe. Trouble and tension have existed in the world since time began—these days are really not that different— and the answers have always been in God's Word. There we find a God who is at once loving and merciful, yet also awesome in power and promising to right all wrongs forever.

v

In this book you will find over two hundred questions on various "touchpoints," topics that may touch your heart during these troubled times. Each topic is listed alphabetically—with questions, Scripture passages, and comments addressing each topic. In the index at the back, you will find a complete listing of all the topics for quick reference. You can read through this book page by page or use it as a reference guide for topics of particular interest to you.

Although we could not cover all topics, questions, and Scriptures related to the subject of this book, our prayer is that you will continue to search God's Word deliberately and diligently. May you find God's answers, for he longs to be your daily guide. Enjoy your treasure hunt!

—THE EDITORS

2 Timothy 3:16-17 *All Scripture is inspired by God and is useful to teach us what is true and to make us realize what is wrong in our lives. It straightens us out and teaches us to do what is right. It is God's way of preparing us in every way, fully equipped for every good thing God wants us to do.*

Absence

Why do I sometimes feel that God is absent? I need to feel him close today, but I don't feel him at all.

Psalm 10:1 *O Lord, why do you stand so far away? Why do you hide when I need you the most?*
The greater your troubles, the farther away God sometimes seems. In your darkest hour, you may feel that God is hiding. You must have faith in his promise to always be with you. Don't trust your feelings; trust God and his promises to you.

Psalm 139:2, 7 *You know when I sit down or stand up. You know my every thought. . . . I can never escape from your spirit! I can never get away from your presence!*
Even though you may feel that God is far away, he is in fact very near to you at all times. No matter how troubled you may feel, trust that God is right there with you. You can never get away from his presence.

1

Psalm 23:4 *Even when I walk through the dark valley of death, I will not be afraid, for you are close beside me.*

God never promised that by believing in him your life would be free from trouble, but he does promise to be with you even in your darkest moments. He does not promise to take you around the dark valley, but he does promise to walk with you through it. This truth does not make these moments easy, but it does enable you to move through them without fear. When you walk through the valley of trouble, suffering, sorrow, or loneliness, remember that God is close beside you.

PROMISE FROM GOD Matthew 28:20 *Be sure of this: I am with you always, even to the end of the age.*

Adversity

Is God listening when I cry out because of my troubles? Does he really hear, and does he care?

Jonah 2:2 *I cried out to the LORD in my great trouble, and he answered me. I called to you from the world of the dead, and LORD, you heard me!*

God's hot line is always open. There is never a busy signal, for he is never too busy with

2

anything—even managing the world—to listen to your every need. God has both a listening ear and a caring heart. And he will answer you.

Will being faithful to God spare me from adversity?

Exodus 5:6-8 *Pharaoh sent this order to the slave drivers. . . . "Do not supply the [Israelites] with any more straw for making bricks. Let them get it themselves! . . . They obviously don't have enough to do. If they did, they wouldn't be talking about going into the wilderness to offer sacrifices to their God."*

When you believe in Jesus, Satan becomes your enemy. He will try to stop you from following God by giving you all manner of adversity. He hopes that he can at least make you doubt God and be unable to witness for him. You must recognize that adversity may be a sign that you are being faithful to God. So continue to be faithful, even through times of adversity.

PROMISE FROM GOD Isaiah 43:2-3 *When you go through deep waters and great trouble, I will be with you. . . . For I am the Lord, your God.*

Assurance

Where can I find assurance amid the uncertainties of life? Can I be sure of anything?

1 Peter 1:21 *Through Christ you have come to trust in God. And because God raised Christ from the dead and gave him great glory, your faith and hope can be placed confidently in God.*

God is the only one in whom you can completely trust without fear of disappointment. You can be assured that what he says is true and what he does is reliable. The world is filled with uncertainty, but you can trust in God's sure promises.

Ephesians 3:12 *Because of Christ and our faith in him, we can now come fearlessly into God's presence, assured of his glad welcome.*

You can approach God knowing that he gladly welcomes you and will never reject you. You can be assured that God always listens, always hears, always loves, is always there.

Romans 8:35, 38-39 *Can anything ever separate us from Christ's love? Does it mean he no longer loves us if we have trouble or calamity? . . . I am convinced that nothing can ever separate us from his love. . . . Our fears for today, our worries about tomorrow, and even the powers of hell can't keep God's love away.*

Life's circumstances don't come between God and his people. You can rest assured that through deep waters and great trouble, he is with you. Nothing can separate you from him.

How can I feel more sure of God's assurances? What can I do to increase my confidence in him?

Psalm 108:1 *My heart is confident in you, O God; no wonder I can sing your praises! Wake up, my soul!*
Praise will increase your assurance. As you focus on the Lord instead of your problems or fears, your confidence in him will increase.

Psalm 34:4 *I prayed to the LORD, and he answered me, freeing me from all my fears.*
Frequent prayer will deepen your assurance. Your conversations with God remind you that he is truly there.

Psalm 40:1, 5 *I waited patiently for the LORD to help me, and he turned to me and heard my cry. . . . O LORD my God, you have done many miracles for us. Your plans for us are too numerous to list.*
Remembering God's faithfulness will increase your assurance. As you depend on God in your everyday life, God develops a track record that makes you more confident as you face today's challenges. What God has done assures you of what he will continue to do.

What difference will it make for me today if I place my full assurance in God?

Psalm 3:5 *I lay down and slept. I woke up in safety, for the LORD was watching over me.*
Placing your assurance in God gives you inner peace regardless of your circumstances. The God of peace is the only reliable source of true peace.

Psalm 27:3 *Though a mighty army surrounds me, my heart will know no fear. Even if they attack me, I remain confident.*

Psalm 56:9 *On the very day I call to you for help, my enemies will retreat. This I know: God is on my side.*
Because of your assurance in God and his promises, you can have confidence to face the challenges of your life.

How can I be sure of God's love for me?

John 3:16 *For God so loved the world that he gave his only Son, so that everyone who believes in him will not perish but have eternal life.*

Romans 5:8 *But God showed his great love for us by sending Christ to die for us while we were still sinners.*
You can have full assurance in God's love because God *is* love. Love is not merely something God does; love is who he is. You can be sure of this love because of what he has done for you— sending his Son to save you.

How can I be sure of God's promises to me?

Psalm 146:6 *He is the one who made heaven and earth, the sea, and everything in them. He is the one who keeps every promise forever.*
You can have assurance in God's promises because God is truth. He cannot and does not lie.

John 10:28-30 *I give them eternal life, and they will never perish. No one will snatch them away from me, for my Father has given them to me, and he is more powerful than anyone else. So no one can take them from me. The Father and I are one.*
God's power gives assurance in his ability to keep his promises. He who made the universe and founded it on truth will certainly keep his promises to you.

2 Corinthians 1:20 *For all of God's promises have been fulfilled in him. That is why we say "Amen" when we give glory to God through Christ.*
Fulfilled prophecies and historical examples are evidence of God's ability to keep his promises. If we trust people because we have seen their track record over a few years, certainly we can trust God because he has a spotless track record from the beginning of time. Fulfilled prophecies affirm God's promises. Because he has always kept his promises, you can trust that he will continue to keep his promises.

PROMISE FROM GOD Jeremiah
17:7-8 *But blessed are those who trust in the LORD and have made the LORD their hope and confidence. They are like trees planted along a riverbank, with roots that reach deep into the water. Such trees are not bothered by the heat or worried by long months of drought. Their leaves stay green, and they go right on producing delicious fruit.*

Blessings

If God promises to bless his people, why is life sometimes so full of trouble?

Acts 5:41 *The apostles left the high council rejoicing that God had counted them worthy to suffer dishonor for the name of Jesus.*

James 1:12 *God blesses the people who patiently endure testing.*

Sometimes great blessings come out of great trouble because these trials deepen your relationship with the Lord, which is the greatest blessing of all.

How can the promise of blessing help me when I am weary or discouraged?

Galatians 6:9 *Don't get tired of doing what is good. Don't get discouraged and give up, for we will reap a harvest of blessing at the appropriate time.*

When you are tempted to give up, new resolve comes from remembering that God promises to bring a harvest of blessing in his perfect time.

Should I bless my enemies?

Romans 12:14 *If people persecute you because you are a Christian, don't curse them; pray that God will bless them.*

Jesus brought a new idea—blessing and forgiveness for enemies. This is unique to Christianity. The natural response toward one's enemies is a desire for revenge. Prayer for your enemies is a severe test of your devotion to Christ.

PROMISE FROM GOD Ephesians 1:3 *How we praise God, the Father of our Lord Jesus Christ, who has blessed us with every spiritual blessing in the heavenly realms because we belong to Christ.*

Brokenhearted

(see also ENCOURAGEMENT or GRIEF or SORROW)

How does God respond to the brokenhearted?

Psalm 34:18 *The LORD is close to the brokenhearted; he rescues those who are crushed in spirit.*

Psalm 147:3 *He heals the brokenhearted, binding up their wounds.*
The Lord comforts the brokenhearted by his presence, his compassion, his listening, his love, his healing, his encouragement, and his blessing. When your heart is broken, so is his.

I am brokenhearted. What should I do?

Psalm 143:7-8 *Come quickly, LORD, and answer me, for my depression deepens. Don't turn away from me, or I will die. Let me hear of your unfailing love to me in the morning, for I am trusting you. Show me where to walk, for I have come to you in prayer.*

Psalm 130:1 *From the depths of despair, O LORD, I call for your help.*
Call to the Lord for his help. Be honest with your feelings. He who made you can heal your broken heart. He who loves you will draw you close.

Psalm 119:28, 50, 52, 92 *I weep with grief; encourage me by your word. . . . Your promise revives me; it comforts me in all my troubles. . . . I meditate on your age-old laws; O LORD, they comfort me. . . . If your law hadn't sustained me with joy, I would have died in my misery.*

Psalm 19:8 *The commandments of the LORD are right, bringing joy to the heart. The commands of the LORD are clear, giving insight to life.*
Look to the Word of God for help. Meditate on God's character, promises, and commitment to

you. He who created the universe by his word can re-create a new spirit within you. His Word will comfort and encourage you.

Mark 14:34-36 *He told them, "My soul is crushed with grief to the point of death. Stay here and watch with me." He went on a little farther and fell face down on the ground. He prayed that, if it were possible, the awful hour awaiting him might pass him by. "Abba, Father," he said, "everything is possible for you. Please take this cup of suffering away from me. Yet I want your will, not mine."* Look to God in honest prayer. Prayer puts you in touch with the source of all healing.

Can God use my broken heart to bring him glory? If so, how might that happen?

Psalm 51:8-10 *Oh, give me back my joy again; you have broken me—now let me rejoice. Don't keep looking at my sins. Remove the stain of my guilt. Create in me a clean heart, O God. Renew a right spirit within me.*

Psalm 30:11 *You have turned my mourning into joyful dancing. You have taken away my clothes of mourning and clothed me with joy.*
Your brokenness leads to healing, and healing leads to rejoicing. When God does his healing in your life, you will rejoice and others will rejoice with you.

2 Corinthians 1:4 *He comforts us in all our troubles so that we can comfort others. When others are troubled, we will be able to give them the same comfort God has given us.*
Your broken heart can help you comfort others. In your brokenness, you understand others who are broken.

Many around me are brokenhearted, Lord. How can I help them?

Romans 12:15 *When others are happy, be happy with them. If they are sad, share their sorrow.*
You can share in others' sorrow as surely as you can share in their joy.

1 Peter 5:12 *I have written this short letter to you with the help of Silas, whom I consider a faithful brother. My purpose in writing is to encourage you and assure you that the grace of God is with you no matter what happens.*
You can encourage the brokenhearted. Words of comfort can lift up the hurting person.

1 Thessalonians 3:7 *We have been greatly comforted, dear brothers and sisters, in all of our own crushing troubles and suffering, because you have remained strong in your faith.*

Romans 1:12 *I'm eager to encourage you in your faith, but I also want to be encouraged by yours. In this way, each of us will be a blessing to the other.*
You can remain strong in your own faith. Those

12

weakened by hurt are encouraged to seek counsel from others who have overcome similar hurt.

PROMISE FROM GOD Psalm 40:2
He lifted me out of the pit of despair, out of the mud and the mire. He set my feet on solid ground and steadied me as I walked along.

Caring

Does God care what happens to me?
Psalm 71:6 *You have been with me from birth; from my mother's womb you have cared for me. No wonder I am always praising you!*

Psalm 31:7 *I am overcome with joy because of your unfailing love, for you have seen my troubles, and you care about the anguish of my soul.*
God's love for you began before you were born, continues throughout your life, and extends through eternity.

How does God show his care for me?
Psalm 121:7-8 *The LORD keeps you from all evil and preserves your life. The LORD keeps watch over you as you come and go, both now and forever.*

Psalm 145:18-20 *The LORD is close to all who call on him, yes, to all who call on him sincerely. He fulfills the desires of those who fear him; he hears their cries for help and rescues them. The* LORD *protects all those who love him, but he destroys the wicked.*

Matthew 6:30 *And if God cares so wonderfully for flowers that are here today and gone tomorrow, won't he more surely care for you? You have so little faith!*
God protects you, provides for your needs, and preserves you—now and forever.

How can I show others I care?

Luke 10:34 *Kneeling beside him, the Samaritan soothed his wounds with medicine and bandaged them.*

Matthew 25:36 *I was naked, and you gave me clothing. I was sick, and you cared for me. I was in prison, and you visited me.*

1 Corinthians 12:25 *This makes for harmony among the members, so that all the members care for each other equally.*
As God shows his care for you by protecting, providing, and preserving, so you can show his care to others by doing the same for them. You can protect by being kind, helpful, and willing to reach out. You can provide by giving of your time, treasure, and talents to those in need. You can preserve by helping to maintain harmony by the words you say and the actions you do.

PROMISE FROM GOD 1 Peter 5:7
Give all your worries and cares to God, for he cares about what happens to you.

Challenges

In a world that seems opposed to God, how do I handle the challenge of keeping my faith strong?

Psalm 40:12 *Troubles surround me—too many to count! They pile up so high I can't see my way out. They are more numerous than the hairs on my head. I have lost all my courage.*

Hebrews 6:18 *God has given us both his promise and his oath. These two things are unchangeable because it is impossible for God to lie. Therefore, we who have fled to him for refuge can take new courage, for we can hold on to his promise with confidence.* The strength to handle challenges comes from God alone. Therefore you must stay close to him through Bible study and prayer, never doubting his promises. When you face opposition, always stand your ground on the truth of God's Word. When you do, you cannot be shaken.

How can I possibly face the challenges of today? I don't think I can make it.

2 Corinthians 1:8-10 *I think you ought*

*to know, dear brothers and sisters, about the trouble
we went through in the province of Asia. We were
crushed and completely overwhelmed, and we thought
we would never live through it. In fact, we expected
to die. But as a result, we learned not to rely on ourselves, but on God who can raise the dead. And he did
deliver us from mortal danger. And we are confident
that he will continue to deliver us.*

When your troubles are overwhelming, you must
continue to look to God and his power to help.
Bravely keep your focus on God and patiently
watch him work.

2 Samuel 22:30 *In your strength I can crush
an army; with my God I can scale any wall.*

Ephesians 3:20 *Now glory be to God! By his
mighty power at work within us, he is able to accomplish infinitely more than we would ever dare to ask
or hope.*

Regardless of the size of the task, God's strength
working in you is sufficient to see his work
through to completion. God will never call
you to a task without going with you to see it
through. He will provide all that you need.

PROMISE FROM GOD Joshua
1:7, 9 *Be strong and very courageous. Obey all the
laws Moses gave you. Do not turn away from them,
and you will be successful in everything you do. . . .
I command you—be strong and courageous! Do not*

be afraid or discouraged. For the LORD your God is with you wherever you go.

Change

With all the change in my life, how can I keep it all together?

Hebrews 1:12 *You [God] are always the same.*

Hebrews 13:8 *Jesus Christ is the same yesterday, today, and forever.*

You can trust the character of God to be unchanging and reliable. No matter how much your life changes, no matter what new situations you face, God goes with you—and he never changes.

Mark 13:31 *Heaven and earth will disappear, but my words will remain forever.*

You can build your life on God's Word because its truth is changeless. As you face change, constantly turn to God's Word to maintain your perspective and to keep you grounded.

Genesis 37:28; 41:39-40 *When the traders came by, his brothers pulled Joseph out of the pit and sold him for twenty pieces of silver. . . .*

Pharaoh said, ". . . I hereby appoint you to direct this project. . . . Only I will have a rank higher than yours."

Romans 8:28 *And we know that God causes everything to work together for the good of those who love God and are called according to his purpose for them.*

Sometimes change seems to be for the worse. At those times, you may feel as if you're going to fall apart. When such change occurs, remember that God can work his will even through traumatic, unpredictable, and unfair change. Nothing takes him by surprise. No change occurs that he cannot redeem.

PROMISE FROM GOD Numbers 23:19 *God is not a man, that he should lie. He is not a human, that he should change his mind. Has he ever spoken and failed to act? Has he ever promised and not carried it through?*

Chaos

The world seems to be in complete chaos. How can I find order and peace in my inner spirit?

2 Peter 1:2 *May God bless you with his special favor and wonderful peace as you come to know Jesus, our God and Lord, better and better.*
Pursue knowing the Lord God, the Creator of order and peace. As you get to know him better, you will be filled with his peace.

Romans 5:1 *Since we have been made right in God's sight by faith, we have peace with God because of what Jesus Christ our Lord has done for us.*

You have been given peace as a result of your relationship with Jesus. So partake of that gift. God is constantly at work to give you inner peace as you follow him.

Psalm 39:2, 7 *As I stood there in silence—not even speaking of good things—the turmoil within me grew to the bursting point. . . . And so, Lord, where do I put my hope? My only hope is in you.*
The troubles in life will always threaten our peace. Various degrees of chaos and turmoil will continue throughout your life. In order to find peace in the chaos, seek to understand God's perspective toward life. He will give you hope.

Romans 16:17 *And now I make one more appeal, my dear brothers and sisters. Watch out for people who cause divisions and upset people's faith by teaching things that are contrary to what you have been taught. Stay away from them.*
Guard what you hear and believe; watch the company that you keep. Chaos is often the result of not being diligent in avoiding that which causes strife and division in your life. Guard carefully the gates to your soul because chaos, like an enemy army, will invade and disrupt your peace and confidence in God.

PROMISE FROM GOD Isaiah 45:18 *For the LORD is God, and he created the heavens and earth and put everything in place. He made the world to be lived in, not to be a place of empty chaos. "I am the LORD," he says, "and there is no other."*

Circumstances

Is God in control of my circumstances?

Psalm 135:6 *The LORD does whatever pleases him throughout all heaven and earth, and on the seas and in their depths.*

Isaiah 45:7 *I am the one who creates the light and makes the darkness. I am the one who sends good times and bad times. I, the LORD, am the one who does these things.*

Not only is God in control of life's circumstances, but he is able to bring good out of any circumstance.

How does God view my circumstances? How should I view my circumstances?

2 Chronicles 32:7-8 *"Be strong and courageous! Don't be afraid of the king of Assyria or his mighty army, for there is a power far greater on our side! He may have a great army, but they are just men. We have the LORD our God to help us and to fight our battles for us!" These words greatly encouraged the people.*

Because you know God, you can view your circumstances with his perspective. Try to understand his ways, his thoughts, his view of your situation. The more you walk in godliness, the more you will see things the way God sees them. The more you avoid godliness, the more you see only your own ways.

Isaiah 45:9 *Destruction is certain for those who argue with their Creator. Does a clay pot ever argue with its maker? Does the clay dispute with the one who shapes it, saying, "Stop, you are doing it wrong!" Does the pot exclaim, "How clumsy can you be!"* View your life's circumstances through the lens of God's design, control, and authority. Did you create the universe? Who did? Did you create your own life? Who did? Can you fully comprehend yourself and your own circumstances? Who can? Only God. Why then would you not want to entrust yourself to him?

Hebrews 11:11-12 *It was by faith that Sarah together with Abraham was able to have a child, even though they were too old and Sarah was barren. Abraham believed that God would keep his promise. And so a whole nation came from this one man, Abraham, who was too old to have any children— a nation with so many people that, like the stars of the sky and the sand on the seashore, there is no way to count them.*
View God working in life's circumstances through eyes and hearts of faith. The "glasses" you wear color the view.

How should I respond to life's sometimes troubling circumstances?

Habakkuk 3:17-19 *Even though the fig trees have no blossoms, and there are no grapes on the vine; even though the olive crop fails, and the fields lie empty and barren; even though the flocks die in the fields, and the cattle barns are empty, yet I will rejoice in the LORD! I will be joyful in the God of my salvation. The Sovereign LORD is my strength! He will make me as surefooted as a deer and bring me safely over the mountains.*

Focus more on the joy, the peace, and the future that come from a relationship with God and less on your troubles. You can always respond joyfully to the God who offers you the eternal gift of salvation. The more you wallow in unpleasant circumstances, the more they may drag you under. The more you reach out to God, the more he can lift you up.

1 Thessalonians 5:18 *No matter what happens, always be thankful, for this is God's will for you who belong to Christ Jesus.*

Accept life's circumstances with thanksgiving to God, as well as trust in him for his constant presence and comfort. Whether you are currently living in sunshine or rain, God never changes and his love for you never changes. God is always eager to teach you something from both the good and the bad.

22

Philippians 4:6 *Don't worry about anything; instead, pray about everything. Tell God what you need, and thank him for all he has done.*

Refuse to worry. One of the hardest lessons of life is to turn worry into confident prayer when bad circumstances come your way. Come to God with your needs, giving thanks for what he has done for you, and trusting that he will bring good out of the difficult.

Jeremiah 42:6 *Whether we like it or not, we will obey the LORD our God to whom we send you with our plea. For if we obey him, everything will turn out well for us.*

Respond in obedience to God in every circumstance. He sees the larger picture and the future.

Philippians 4:11-13 *Not that I was ever in need, for I have learned how to get along happily whether I have much or little. I know how to live on almost nothing or with everything. I have learned the secret of living in every situation, whether it is with a full stomach or empty, with plenty or little. For I can do everything with the help of Christ who gives me the strength I need.*

Respond with confidence in God's strength.

How can I make the most of my circumstances?

Jeremiah 17:7-8 *Blessed are those who trust in the LORD and have made the LORD their hope and* *confidence. They are like trees planted along a river-bank, with roots that reach deep into the water. Such trees are not bothered by the heat or worried by long months of drought. Their leaves stay green, and they go right on producing delicious fruit.*

Trust in the Lord; he is worthy of your hope and confidence. Those who trust in the Lord understand the secret of his life-sustaining power.

Esther 4:13-14 *Mordecai sent back this reply to Esther: "Don't think for a moment that you will escape there in the palace when all other Jews are killed. If you keep quiet at a time like this, deliverance for the Jews will arise from some other place, but you and your relatives will die. What's more, who can say but that you have been elevated to the palace for just such a time as this?"*

God can use you as you are. Start with who you are and what you have, not with who you wish you were and what you don't have. Seek to obey God in your current circumstances. God may have you there for "such a time as this."

James 1:2-3 *Dear brothers and sisters, whenever trouble comes your way, let it be an opportunity for joy. For when your faith is tested, your endurance has a chance to grow.*

You can experience joy and growth in difficult circumstances. Plants continue to grow even on cloudy days. Life can continue to flourish despite cloudy circumstances.

Acts 16:25 *Around midnight, Paul and Silas were praying and singing hymns to God, and the other prisoners were listening.*
You can glorify God even in the most difficult of circumstances. When you do, two wonderful things happen: you learn to rely on God and not yourself, and others are blessed by seeing your faith and hope in action.

How does God use circumstances for my good?

Romans 5:3 *We can rejoice, too, when we run into problems and trials, for we know that they are good for us—they help us learn to endure.*
God uses your circumstances for your own personal growth—for your good. You won't always know why God sometimes allows bad circumstances to come your way, but you can know for sure that God always wants to bring good out of the bad. That's why you can confidently rejoice, even in problems and trials, for God is working in you to make you stronger and more Christlike.

Philippians 1:12-14 *And I want you to know, dear brothers and sisters, that everything that has happened to me here has helped to spread the Good News. For everyone here, including all the soldiers in the palace guard, knows that I am in chains because of Christ. And because of my imprisonment, many of the Christians here have gained confidence and become more bold in telling others about Christ.* God uses your circumstances to help you grow. Then you can help others grow. Anyone can be joyful and faithful when life is going well, but when life gets tough believers have a unique opportunity to show how a relationship with God brings comfort, confidence, and hope.

How can I see God when things look bad?

Psalm 16:8 *I know the LORD is always with me. I will not be shaken, for he is right beside me.* If God went to such great trouble to create us and a world for us to live in, send his Son to die for our sins, and prepare an eternal home for us in heaven, why would he abandon us in our day-to-day circumstances? Pray for his intervention and then watch closely for God's presence and his power in your life.

PROMISE FROM GOD Psalm 112:4, 6-8 *When darkness overtakes the godly, light will come bursting in. They are generous, compassionate, and righteous. . . . Such people will not be overcome by evil circumstances. Those who are righteous will be long remembered. They do not fear bad news; they confidently trust the LORD to care for them. They are confident and fearless and can face their foes triumphantly.*

Comfort

In my times of distress, will God comfort me?

2 Chronicles 15:4 *But whenever you were in distress and turned to the LORD, the God of Israel, and sought him out, you found him.*
Your need for comfort and God's supply of comfort are always in perfect balance.

Isaiah 40:11 *He will feed his flock like a shepherd. He will carry the lambs in his arms . . . [and] gently lead the mother sheep with their young.*
God has a shepherd's heart. You are his lamb, weak and discouraged, carried in his arms.

Psalm 119:52 *I meditate on your age-old laws; O LORD, they comfort me.*

2 Thessalonians 2:16-17 *May our Lord Jesus Christ . . . who . . . gave us everlasting comfort and good hope, comfort your hearts and give you strength in every good thing you do and say.*
Since God is your ultimate comfort, his Word is your greatest resource for comfort. God's Word is as close as your fingertips, and God himself is as close as your whispered prayer.

In what ways will I receive comfort from God?

Matthew 5:4 *God blesses those who mourn, for they will be comforted.*
You will receive comfort when you grieve.

Exodus 14:13 *But Moses told the people, "Don't be afraid. Just stand where you are and watch the LORD rescue you."*
You will receive comfort when you are overwhelmed.

John 16:33 *Here on earth you will have many trials and sorrows. But take heart, because I have overcome the world.*
You will receive comfort when you are persecuted.

Isaiah 41:10 *Don't be afraid, for I am with you. Do not be dismayed, for I am your God. I will strengthen you. I will help you. I will uphold you with my victorious right hand.*
You will receive comfort when you are rejected.

Psalm 138:3 *When I pray, you answer me; you encourage me by giving me the strength I need.*
You will receive comfort in the midst of conflict.

Genesis 26:24 *Do not be afraid, for I am with you and will bless you.*
You will receive comfort when you are afraid.

How does God comfort me?

Romans 8:26 *And the Holy Spirit helps us in our distress. For we don't even know what we should pray for, nor how we should pray. But the Holy Spirit prays for us with groanings that cannot be expressed in words.*
He prays for you.

Psalm 10:17 *LORD, you know the hopes of the helpless. Surely you will listen to their cries and comfort them.*
He listens to you.

Psalm 94:19 *When doubts filled my mind, your comfort gave me renewed hope and cheer.*
He gives you hope and cheer.

Psalm 119:50,52 *Your promise revives me; it comforts me in all my troubles. . . . I meditate on your age-old laws; O LORD, they comfort me.*
He revives you with his Word.

Psalm 119:76 *Now let your unfailing love comfort me, just as you promised me, your servant.*
He loves you.

2 Thessalonians 2:16-17 *May our Lord Jesus Christ and God our Father, who loved us and in his special favor gave us everlasting comfort and good hope, comfort your hearts and give you strength in every good thing you do and say.*
He gives you eternal hope.

How can I comfort others?

2 Corinthians 1:3-4 *All praise to the God and Father of our Lord Jesus Christ. He is the source of every mercy and the God who comforts us. . . . When others are troubled, we will be able to give them the same comfort God has given us.*
By understanding.

Job 42:11 *Then all his brothers, sisters, and former friends came and feasted with him in his home. And they consoled him and comforted him because of all the trials the LORD had brought against him. And each of them brought him a gift of money and a gold ring.*
By being present.

Job 21:2 *Listen closely to what I am saying. You can console me by listening to me.*
By listening.

Ruth 2:13 *"I hope I continue to please you, sir," she replied. "You have comforted me by speaking so kindly to me, even though I am not as worthy as your workers."*
By your words.

Philemon 1:7 *I myself have gained much joy and comfort from your love, my brother, because your kindness has so often refreshed the hearts of God's people.*
By your love expressed through kindness.

PROMISE FROM GOD 2 Thessalonians 2:16-17 *May our Lord Jesus Christ . . . who . . . gave us everlasting comfort and good hope, comfort your hearts and give you strength in every good thing you do and say.*

Confusion

The world is a pretty confusing place right now. How should I deal with life's confusion?

Joshua 7:6-8 *Joshua and the leaders of Israel tore their clothing in dismay, threw dust on their heads, and bowed down facing the Ark of the LORD until evening. Then Joshua cried out, "Sovereign LORD, why did you bring us across the Jordan River if you are going to let the Amorites kill us? If only we had been content to stay on the other side! Lord, what am I to say, now that Israel has fled from its enemies?"*

Psalm 94:19 *When doubts filled my mind, your comfort gave me renewed hope and cheer.*
As you focus your time and thoughts on God, it becomes clear what he wants you to do. The confusion doesn't seem so great because he is the God of order and peace. Life is less confusing when you realize he truly is in control. How wonderful to know that when you are confused, God has an answer. Just ask.

Psalm 75:3 *When the earth quakes and its people live in turmoil, I am the one who keeps its foundations firm.*
As a believer, you can trust God and recognize his sovereignty. With the help of a sovereign God, confusion seems manageable. You know

that one day God will take away all the confusion and bring his kingdom of peace.

Proverbs 20:24 *How can we understand the
road we travel? It is the LORD who directs our steps.*
Seeing life through your limited vision brings
confusion and frustration. Ask God for understanding. His wisdom will help you sort out the
confusion.

2 Timothy 3:16 *All Scripture is inspired by
God and is useful to teach us what is true and to
make us realize what is wrong in our lives. It
straightens us out and teaches us to do what is right.*
Look to Scripture for instruction and understanding. God will give you wisdom to deal with
any situation. Through the Word of God you
discover the mind of God.

John 16:13 *When the Spirit of truth comes, he
will guide you into all truth. He will not be presenting
his own ideas; he will be telling you what he has
heard. He will tell you about the future.*
Be sensitive to the Holy Spirit. He gives the power
to deal with confusion. Since you don't know the
mysteries of life, you need the one who understands and knows all things to guide you.

2 Corinthians 4:8 *We are pressed on every
side by troubles, but we are not crushed and broken.
We are perplexed, but we don't give up and quit.*
When you refuse to give up and quit, you

continue to grow toward spiritual maturity. As you mature in Christ, you can learn to better handle the confusing things of life.

How can I avoid feeling constantly confused?

1 Kings 18:21 *Then Elijah stood in front of them and said, "How long are you going to waver between two opinions? If the LORD is God, follow him! But if Baal is God, then follow him!" But the people were completely silent.*
Be a devoted follower of God—constantly and deliberately deciding to trust him and follow his Word, which gives you focus and purpose.

How should I respond when God confuses me—when I don't understand him?

Hebrews 10:23 *Without wavering, let us hold tightly to the hope we say we have, for God can be trusted to keep his promise.*
Trust God and trust that what he says in his Word is true. If that is your compass for direction in life, you will always know what to do and which way to go. It is when you doubt God that life gets confusing.

Acts 10:19 *Meanwhile, as Peter was puzzling over the vision, the Holy Spirit said to him, "Three men have come looking for you."*
Be sensitive to the Holy Spirit.

1 Peter 1:10 *This salvation was something the prophets wanted to know more about. They prophesied about this gracious salvation prepared for you, even though they had many questions as to what it all could mean.*
Respond in obedience regardless of your level of understanding. You need not know everything about plumbing to take a bath. You need not know everything about God to follow him.

Habakkuk 2:1 *I will climb up into my watchtower now and wait to see what the LORD will say to me and how he will answer my complaint.*
Wait for God to answer. Realize that the timing and level of the answer is up to his discretion. Rest in the knowledge that the Lord is God and he is acting in your best interests. The timing of answered prayer is as significant as the answer itself.

PROMISE FROM GOD 1 Corinthians 14:33 *God is not a God of disorder but of peace.*

Convictions

How can I develop godly convictions?
Proverbs 2:8-9 *He guards the paths of justice and protects those who are faithful to him. Then you will understand what is right, just, and fair, and*

you will know how to find the right course of action every time.
Be devoted to God.

Isaiah 51:7 *Listen to me, you who know right from wrong and cherish my law in your hearts. Do not be afraid of people's scorn or their slanderous talk.* Listen to God's commands. You are not to fear other people's voiced or silent opinions.

Psalm 37:30 *The godly offer good counsel; they know what is right from wrong.*
Seek godly counsel.

Why is it important to have convictions? How do godly convictions help me?

Romans 14:22-23 *You may have the faith to believe that there is nothing wrong with what you are doing, but keep it between yourself and God. Blessed are those who do not condemn themselves by doing something they know is all right. But if people have doubts about whether they should eat something, they shouldn't eat it. They would be condemned for not acting in faith before God. If you do anything you believe is not right, you are sinning.*
Living by your convictions can keep you from sinning.

Daniel 1:8 *But Daniel made up his mind not to defile himself by eating the food and wine given to them by the king. He asked the chief official for permission to eat other things instead.*

Living by your convictions helps you resist temptation.

Ezra 4:3 *But Zerubbabel, Jeshua, and the other leaders of Israel replied, "You may have no part in this work, for we have nothing in common. We alone will build the Temple for the LORD, the God of Israel, just as King Cyrus of Persia commanded us."*
Holding to your convictions helps you avoid potentially compromising situations.

Exodus 20:6 *But I lavish my love on those who love me and obey my commands, even for a thousand generations.*
Having godly convictions helps you experience God's love.

Psalm 17:15 *But because I have done what is right, I will see you. When I awake, I will be fully satisfied, for I will see you face to face.*
Having godly convictions helps make you certain about your salvation.

1 John 3:21 *Dear friends, if our conscience is clear, we can come to God with bold confidence.*
Having godly convictions helps you to confidently approach God.

Daniel 1:17, 20 *God gave these four young men an unusual aptitude for learning the literature and science of the time. And God gave Daniel special ability in understanding the meanings of visions and dreams. . . . In all matters requiring wisdom and* *balanced judgment, the king found the advice of these young men to be ten times better than that of all the magicians and enchanters in his entire kingdom.*

Having godly convictions brings wisdom as a reward and by-product.

Ephesians 4:13-15 *We will be mature and full grown in the Lord, measuring up to the full stature of Christ. Then we will no longer be like children, forever changing our minds about what we believe because someone has told us something different or because someone has cleverly lied to us and made the lie sound like the truth. Instead, we will hold to the truth in love, becoming more and more in every way like Christ, who is the head of his body, the church.*

As you lovingly hold to the truth, you will become more like Christ.

PROMISE FROM GOD 1 Corinthians 16:13 *Be on guard. Stand true to what you believe. Be courageous. Be strong.*

Coping

How do I cope when life's pain becomes overwhelming?

Psalm 145:14 *The LORD helps the fallen and lifts up those bent beneath their loads.*

When you are overwhelmed, God is there with mercy and comfort. Alone, you are downcast; with God, you are uplifted.

Isaiah 43:2 *When you go through deep waters and great trouble, I will be with you. When you go through rivers of difficulty, you will not drown! When you walk through the fire of oppression, you will not be burned up; the flames will not consume you.* When you are overwhelmed, God is there with power to help you. Alone, you will drown in deep waters of difficulty; with God, you will prevail.

Psalm 55:2 *Please listen and answer me, for I am overwhelmed by my troubles.*

Psalm 61:2 *From the ends of the earth, I will cry to you for help, for my heart is overwhelmed. Lead me to the towering rock of safety.* When you are overwhelmed, go to God in prayer. When the whole world seems to ignore you, God listens.

Psalm 55:22 *Give your burdens to the LORD, and he will take care of you. He will not permit the godly to slip and fall.* When you are overwhelmed, trust God to care for you.

Psalm 71:14 *But I will keep on hoping for you to help me; I will praise you more and more.*

Psalm 42:5-6 *Why am I discouraged? Why so sad? I will put my hope in God! I will praise him again—my Savior and my God!*
When you are overwhelmed, hope in God and praise him.

Psalm 126:5-6 *Those who plant in tears will harvest with shouts of joy. They weep as they go to plant their seed, but they sing as they return with the harvest.*

Psalm 30:11-12 *You have turned my mourning into joyful dancing. You have taken away my clothes of mourning and clothed me with joy, that I might sing praises to you and not be silent. O LORD my God, I will give you thanks forever!*
When you are overwhelmed, have confidence that you will recover with the Lord's help. With God, even the bitter seeds of tears, grief, and mourning may yield a harvest of joy and blessing.

How do I cope when life's demands seem impossible?

Matthew 19:26 *Jesus looked at them intently and said, "Humanly speaking, it is impossible. But with God everything is possible."*

Philippians 4:13 *For I can do everything with the help of Christ who gives me the strength I need.*
Remember: what seems impossible for you is never impossible for God.

Psalm 39:7 *And so, Lord, where do I put my hope? My only hope is in you.*
Remember: your ultimate hope should not be in anyone or anything other than the Lord. He alone can bring you through the pain safely to the other side.

Genesis 24:12 *"O LORD, God of my master,"* he prayed. *"Give me success and show kindness to my master, Abraham. Help me to accomplish the purpose of my journey."*
Remember: you can pray to God.

Exodus 18:21-23 *Find some capable, honest men who fear God and hate bribes. Appoint them as judges. . . . They will help you carry the load, making the task easier for you. If you follow this advice, and if God directs you to do so, then you will be able to endure the pressures, and all these people will go home in peace.*
Remember: it is important to follow God's directions. Many times seeking godly advice may provide a workable solution you had not considered. God's wisdom may flow to you through godly counselors.

1 Chronicles 28:20 *Then David continued, "Be strong and courageous, and do the work. Don't be afraid or discouraged by the size of the task, for the LORD God, my God, is with you. He will not fail you or forsake you. He will see to it that all the work related to the Temple of the LORD is finished correctly."*

Remember: you can be strong, courageous, steady, enthusiastic, and confident of the Lord's presence. The demands of God's work are often great, but when God is with you, you have reason to be strong and courageous.

How can I help others cope?

2 Corinthians 1:4 *He comforts us in all our troubles so that we can comfort others. When others are troubled, we will be able to give them the same comfort God has given us.*
Be sensitive to those God brings into your life. He often provides opportunities for you to comfort others in circumstances similar to your own.

Romans 15:30 *Dear brothers and sisters, I urge you in the name of our Lord Jesus Christ to join me in my struggle by praying to God for me. Do this because of your love for me, given to you by the Holy Spirit.* Pray for them.

Job 42:11 *Then all his brothers, sisters, and former friends came and feasted with him in his home. And they consoled him and comforted him because of all the trials the LORD had brought against him. And each of them brought him a gift of money and a gold ring.*
Be present for those in need. There is a power of presence that exceeds even the power of words.

Job 21:2 *Listen closely to what I am saying. You can console me by listening to me.*

Listen to those who are struggling. A listening ear reflects a caring heart.

1 Corinthians 9:22 *When I am with those who are oppressed, I share their oppression so that I might bring them to Christ. Yes, I try to find common ground with everyone so that I might bring them to Christ.*
Empathize with others. A sympathetic heart recognizes another's problems; an empathetic heart shares those problems and helps bring others to Christ.

Proverbs 12:25 *Worry weighs a person down; an encouraging word cheers a person up.*

Proverbs 15:23 *Everyone enjoys a fitting reply; it is wonderful to say the right thing at the right time!*

Proverbs 25:11 *Timely advice is as lovely as golden apples in a silver basket.*

Ephesians 4:29 *Let everything you say be good and helpful, so that your words will be an encouragement to those who hear them.*
Speak words that are encouraging, fitting, timely, good, and helpful.

Titus 3:14 *Our people should not have unproductive lives. They must learn to do good by helping others who have urgent needs.*
Be practical in meeting others' needs.

PROMISE FROM GOD Isaiah 40:29 *He gives power to those who are tired and worn out; he offers strength to the weak.*

Courage

Where do I get the courage to go on when life seems too hard or obstacles seem too big?

Psalm 27:1 *The LORD is my light and my salvation—so why should I be afraid?*

Isaiah 41:10 *Don't be afraid, for I am with you. Do not be dismayed, for I am your God. I will strengthen you. I will help you. I will uphold you with my victorious right hand.*

True courage comes from knowing God and understanding that he is stronger than your mightiest foes and he wants to help you. Courage is not misplaced confidence in your weakness, but well-placed confidence in God's strength.

How do I find the courage to face death?

Luke 12:4 *Dear friends, don't be afraid of those who want to kill you. They can only kill the body; they cannot do any more to you.*

When God is with you, you don't have to be afraid of anything, even death.

1 Corinthians 15:54 *Death is swallowed up in victory.*

By his resurrection, Jesus has won the victory over death. Victory over death comes not from a futile attempt to conquer death, but from surrender to Jesus, who promises resurrection and eternal life.

How do I find the courage to face change?

Genesis 46:3 *Do not be afraid to go down to Egypt, for I will see to it that you become a great nation there.*

Change may be part of God's plan for you. If so, what you are headed into will give you joy and satisfaction beyond your expectations. Remember, the greatest advances in life come through change.

Exodus 4:13 *But Moses again pleaded, "Lord, please! Send someone else."*

To experience fear is normal. To be paralyzed by fear, however, can be an indication that you doubt God's ability to care for you in the face of change.

2 Samuel 4:1 *When Ishbosheth heard about Abner's death at Hebron, he lost all courage, and his people were paralyzed with fear.*

If you take all of your courage from another person, you will eventually be left with nothing when that person is gone. If you trust in God, you will have the strength to go on even when circumstances collapse around you.

PROMISE FROM GOD Job 11:18 *You will have courage because you will have hope.*

Crisis

(*see also* ADVERSITY or TROUBLED TIMES)

Where is God in my time of crisis?

Psalm 40:2 *He lifted me out of the pit of despair, out of the mud and the mire. He set my feet on solid ground and steadied me as I walked along.*
You need not pray for the Lord to be with you in your time of crisis—he is already there! Instead, pray that you will recognize his presence and depend on him for help.

John 16:33 *I [Jesus] have told you all this so that you may have peace in me. Here on earth you will have many trials and sorrows. But take heart, because I have overcome the world.*
God does not say he will always prevent crisis in our lives—we all live in a sinful world where terrible things happen—but God does promise to always be there with you, helping you through any crisis. Trust in his promises. Take heart in his presence.

How should I respond to my crisis?

Jonah 2:1 *Then Jonah prayed to the LORD his God from inside the fish.*

Jonah 2:7 *When I had lost all hope, I turned my thoughts once more to the LORD.*

Psalm 57:1 *Have mercy on me, O God, have mercy! I look to you for protection. I will hide beneath the shadow of your wings until this violent storm is past.*
When a crisis leaves you vulnerable and exposed, seek the merciful, protective covering of the Lord himself.

Psalm 130:1 *From the depths of despair, O LORD, I call for your help.*
When you reach the end of your rope, call upon the Lord. Your weaknesses are times for his strength; your crises are his opportunities.

Psalm 28:7 *The LORD is my strength, my shield from every danger. I trust in him with all my heart.*
In a time of crisis you may wonder, *Who can I trust?* You can always trust the Lord.

Psalm 119:143 *As pressure and stress bear down on me, I find joy in your commands.*
When crises seek to undermine you, look to God's Word to undergird you.

What are some of the blessings that can come from my time of crisis?

Jonah 1:16 *The sailors were awestruck by the LORD's great power, and they offered him a sacrifice and vowed to serve him.*
Sometimes a crisis helps you see God more clearly.

Philippians 1:12 *I want you to know, dear brothers and sisters, that everything that has happened to me here has helped to spread the Good News.* How you react to times of crisis can determine what others think about Christ.

Romans 5:3-4 *We can rejoice, too, when we run into problems and trials, for we know that they are good for us—they help us learn to endure. And endurance develops strength of character in us, and character strengthens our confident expectation of salvation.* Times of crisis can strengthen your character.

2 Corinthians 12:10 *Since I know it is all for Christ's good, I am quite content with my weaknesses and with insults, hardships, persecutions, and calamities. For when I am weak, then I am strong.* Times of crisis show clearly that you cannot always rely on your own strength to see you through. You need God's strength. Spiritual strength can grow from physical weakness.

1 Peter 1:6-7 *So be truly glad! There is wonderful joy ahead, even though it is necessary for you to endure many trials for a while. These trials are only to test your faith, to show that it is strong and pure.* Times of crisis test and strengthen your faith.

1 Peter 4:13 *These trials will make you partners with Christ in his suffering.* Times of crisis help you identify with the suffering that Jesus endured for your sake.

How can I help others in their times of crisis?

Proverbs 27:10 *Never abandon a friend— either yours or your father's. Then in your time of need, you won't have to ask your relatives for assistance. It is better to go to a neighbor than to a relative who lives far away.*

1 Corinthians 9:22 *When I am with those who are oppressed, I share their oppression so that I might bring them to Christ. Yes, I try to find common ground with everyone so that I might bring them to Christ.*

When others face crises, you need to be there with them. The power of your presence may comfort them more than the eloquence of your words.

PROMISE FROM GOD Psalm 46:1 *God is our refuge and strength, always ready to help in times of trouble.*

Death

In what way does accepting Christ keep me from dying?

Romans 8:10 *Since Christ lives within you, even though your body will die because of sin, your spirit is alive because you have been made right with God.*

When you accept Christ, you are given eternal life. This does not prevent the death of your body, but it does assure true life with him in heaven forever and ever. And isn't that the life that counts the most?

How do I keep a proper perspective about death? Why am I so afraid of it?

Colossians 3:1-2 *Since you have been raised to new life with Christ, set your sights on the realities of heaven. . . . Let heaven fill your thoughts.*

2 Corinthians 5:4 *We want to slip into our new bodies so that these dying bodies will be swallowed up by everlasting life.*

Fear of the unknown is natural, and fear of death can be healthy if it draws you to know more about God. It is helpful to think of death as a beginning, not an end. It is your entrance into eternal life with God.

Philippians 1:21 *For to me, living is for Christ, and dying is even better.*

A fear of death may be an indication of a weak relationship with God. You must be ready to die—looking forward to being in the presence of the Lord Jesus—in order to appreciate life fully.

Is death really the end?

John 11:25-26 *Jesus told her, "I am the resurrection and the life. Those who believe in me, even*

49

though they die like everyone else, will live again. They are given eternal life for believing in me and will never perish."

1 Corinthians 15:54-55 *When this happens—when our perishable earthly bodies have been transformed into heavenly bodies that will never die—then at last the Scriptures will come true: "Death is swallowed up in victory. O death, where is your victory? O death, where is your sting?"*
For those who trust in Christ, death is not the end, but only the beginning of an eternity of infinite joy with the Lord.

How can I be certain that there is eternal life?

1 Corinthians 15:20 *But the fact is that Christ has been raised from the dead. He has become the first of a great harvest of those who will be raised to life again.*
Resurrection life is not just a theory. Jesus' resurrection guarantees the resurrection of everyone who trusts in him.

1 Corinthians 15:4-6 *He was buried, and he was raised from the dead on the third day, as the Scriptures said. He was seen by Peter and then by the twelve apostles. After that, he was seen by more than five hundred of his followers at one time, most of whom are still alive, though some have died by now.*
The resurrection of Jesus is not mere religious

myth. The biblical record mentions eyewitnesses to the risen Jesus and encourages people to interview them. Historical investigation serves only to confirm the fact of the resurrection. This, in turn, assures you of your eternal life.

What about people who haven't put their faith in Jesus? Is there any hope for them when they die?

John 3:16 *For God so loved the world that he gave his only Son, so that everyone who believes in him will not perish, but have eternal life.*
The only guarantee of eternal life is believing in Jesus. It is wise to examine your own heart and to be sure that you truly believe.

Luke 23:42-43 *Then he said, "Jesus, remember me when you come into your Kingdom." And Jesus replied, "I assure you, today you will be with me in paradise."*
Even at the last minute anyone can receive Jesus' assurance of eternal life as the thief did in Luke's Gospel above. Since you do not know another person's every thought, there is always hope that a person might have turned to the Lord in the last minutes of life.

PROMISE FROM GOD Psalm 49:15 *But as for me, God will redeem my life. He will snatch me from the power of death.*

Depression

(*see also* DISCOURAGEMENT or SORROW)

I feel depressed and it seems like God doesn't care. Does he care about how low I feel?

Psalm 139:12 *Even in darkness I cannot hide from you.*
There is no depth to which you can descend where God is not present with you. When depression comes, you must remember that even though you cannot see or feel his presence, he has not abandoned you.

Psalm 130:1 *From the depths of despair, O LORD, I call for your help.*
You can cry out to God in prayer even during the darkest night of despair. He will hear you.

Isaiah 53:3 *He was despised and rejected— a man of sorrows, acquainted with bitterest grief.*
Remember that Christ understands the pain of human life.

Matthew 11:28 *Jesus said, "Come to me, all of you who are weary and carry heavy burdens, and I will give you rest."*
Jesus cares deeply for the weary and provides acceptance, love, and rest.

Romans 8:39 *Nothing in all creation will ever be*

*able to separate us from the love of God that is
revealed in Christ Jesus our Lord.*
Not even life's worst depression can separate you
from the love of Christ.

How should I handle depression?

Psalm 143:7 *Come quickly, LORD, and answer
me, for my depression deepens. Don't turn away from
me, or I will die.*
The Lord's strong presence in your life is the best
cure for depression. But with the Lord's help, you
may also seek the best medical help and ask God
to use it to heal you.

How does God bring healing to those who
are depressed?

Psalm 10:17 *LORD, you know the hopes of the
helpless. Surely you will listen to their cries and
comfort them.*

Psalm 23:4 *Even when I walk through the dark
valley of death, I will not be afraid, for you are close
beside me. Your rod and your staff protect and
comfort me.*
The power of the Lord's presence, coupled with
the sensitivity of his listening ear, can bring
healing and comfort.

Can any good come out of depression?

Psalm 126:5 *Those who plant in tears will
harvest with shouts of joy.*

2 Corinthians 12:9 *My power works best in your weakness.*

When you are weak, you may be more receptive to the Lord's strength. When God works through your weakness, you know it is his work and not yours.

How can I help someone who is depressed?

2 Corinthians 1:4 *He comforts us in all our troubles so that we can comfort others. When others are troubled, we will be able to give them the same comfort God has given us.*

Romans 12:15 *When others are happy, be happy with them. If they are sad, share their sorrow.*

Proverbs 25:20 *Singing cheerful songs to a person whose heart is heavy is as bad as stealing someone's jacket in cold weather or rubbing salt in a wound.*

Two things help most: modeling the gentle, caring love of Christ and directing the depressed person to the proper care. Those dealing with depression need comfort and understanding, not advice and lectures. You can help someone who is depressed by your quiet presence, your love, and your encouragement. Telling them to "snap out of it" only makes things worse.

Are feelings of depression sin?

Isaiah 24:16 *Listen to them as they sing to the LORD from the ends of the earth. Hear them singing praises to the Righteous One! But my heart is heavy with grief. I am discouraged, for evil still prevails, and treachery is everywhere.*

The flames of moral outrage at the presence of terrible sin can leave the ashes of depression. This is not a sin.

John 11:33 *When Jesus saw her weeping and saw the other people wailing with her, he was moved with indignation and was deeply troubled.*

John 12:27 *Now my soul is deeply troubled. Should I pray, "Father, save me from what lies ahead"? But that is the very reason why I came!*

In the very process of redemption Jesus felt deeply troubled, or quite "low." It is natural to feel low in the backwash of troubled times. Since Jesus cannot sin, to feel low or depressed cannot be a sin. It can be a result of sin or become a sin if you blame God, use it against God, or leave God out of the antidote.

Does feeling depressed mean something is wrong with my faith?

Judges 15:18 *Now Samson was very thirsty, and he cried out to the LORD, "You have accomplished this great victory. . . . Must I now die of thirst?"*

1 Kings 19:3-4 *Elijah was afraid and fled for his life. . . . He sat down under a solitary broom tree and prayed that he might die.*

Even for the people of God, depression can often follow great achievement or spiritual victory.

Psalm 35:9 *I will be glad because he rescues me.*

Psalm 40:2 *He lifted me out of the pit of despair.*

Matthew 14:30-31 *When he looked around at the high waves, he was terrified and began to sink. "Save me, Lord!" he shouted. Instantly Jesus reached out his hand and grabbed him.*
God is able to lift you out of the pit of depression and fear.

PROMISE FROM GOD Matthew 11:28 *Then Jesus said, "Come to me, all of you who are weary and carry heavy burdens, and I will give you rest."*

Despair / Desperation

I sometimes think I'm losing it. The pain is so intense, the hurt so deep. How can God help me in this time of despair?

Psalm 102:17 *He will listen to the prayers of the destitute. He will not reject their pleas.*

Psalm 130:1 *From the depths of despair, O LORD, I call for your help.*

2 Samuel 22:7 *But in my distress I cried out to the LORD; yes, I called to my God for help. He heard me from his sanctuary; my cry reached his ears.*

God listens and cares about you, so never stop talking to him through prayer.

Psalm 39:7 *And so, Lord, where do I put my hope? My only hope is in you.*

Psalm 42:5 *Why am I discouraged? Why so sad? I will put my hope in God! I will praise him again— my Savior and my God!*
God heals your heart.

John 11:4 *When Jesus heard about it he said, "Lazarus's sickness will not end in death. No, it is for the glory of God. I, the Son of God, will receive glory from this."*
God sends his help no matter how hopeless the circumstances seem. He is the God of the impossible.

Romans 8:26 *And the Holy Spirit helps us in our distress. For we don't even know what we should pray for, nor how we should pray. But the Holy Spirit prays for us with groanings that cannot be expressed in words.*
God gives his Spirit as your personal intercessor. When you can't even form the words of your prayer, let the Holy Spirit intercede for you. He can pray for you when you don't even know what to pray for yourself.

Psalm 119:43,49 *Do not snatch your word of truth from me, for my only hope is in your laws. . . . Remember your promise to me, for it is my only hope.*
God gives his Word, full of his promises. Read it!

Isaiah 61:3 *To all who mourn in Israel, he will give beauty for ashes, joy instead of mourning, praise instead of despair. For the LORD has planted them like strong and graceful oaks for his own glory.*

Jeremiah 29:11 *"I know the plans I have for you," says the LORD. "They are plans for good and not for disaster, to give you a future and a hope."*
God gives a hope-filled future. Depend on him!

PROMISE FROM GOD: 1 Peter 5:7
Give all your worries and cares to God, for he cares about what happens to you.

Disappointment

How should I handle my disappointment with God?

Exodus 5:22 *So Moses went back to the LORD and protested.*
Go to God in prayer to try to understand his ways.

John 11:21 *Martha said to Jesus, "Lord, if you had been here, my brother would not have died."*
Be honest with God about your thoughts and feelings. He knows them anyway, so why try to hide them?

2 Corinthians 12:8-10 *Three different times I begged the Lord to take it away. Each time he said, "My gracious favor is all you need. My power works*

best in your weakness." So now I am glad to boast about my weaknesses, so that the power of Christ may work through me. . . . For when I am weak, then I am strong.

Remember that although you may not understand why God doesn't always take away your pain, your weaknesses are great opportunities for God to work his power through you.

How should I deal with life's disappointments?

Psalm 63:1 *O God, you are my God; I earnestly search for you. My soul thirsts for you.*

In your disappointment, move toward God, not away from him. Running from the one who can help you is not wise.

Luke 5:4-5 *When he had finished speaking, he said to Simon, "Now go out where it is deeper and let down your nets, and you will catch many fish." "Master," Simon replied, "we worked hard all last night and didn't catch a thing. But if you say so, we'll try again."*

Listen to the Lord and trust him, even when it seems unreasonable.

Romans 8:28 *And we know that God causes everything to work together for the good of those who love God and are called according to his purpose for them.*

Accept God's ability to still bring good.

Is there a way to avoid or minimize disappointment?

Haggai 1:6, 9 *You have planted much but harvested little. . . . Why? Because my house lies in ruins, says the LORD Almighty, while you are all busy building your own fine houses.*
Put God first. Give him the first part of your money, the best minutes of your day, the highest priority in your life. By doing this, you will learn to see what is truly important, and you will discover that there is nothing more rewarding and satisfying than a relationship with the God who created you and loves you.

1 Peter 2:6 *As the Scriptures express it, "I am placing a stone in Jerusalem, a chosen cornerstone, and anyone who believes in him will never be disappointed."*
Put your faith, trust, and expectations in the Lord. Because he created you, you can only learn from him what he has planned for you.

Galatians 6:9 *So don't get tired of doing what is good. Don't get discouraged and give up, for we will reap a harvest of blessing at the appropriate time.*
Maintain the joy of doing God's good work.

Galatians 6:4 *Be sure to do what you should, for then you will enjoy the personal satisfaction of having done your work well, and you won't need to compare yourself to anyone else.*

Minimize disappointment by doing what you should—and doing it well.

PROMISE FROM GOD Psalm 55:22
Give your burdens to the LORD, and he will take care of you.

Discouragement

(*see also* DEPRESSION or ENCOURAGEMENT or SORROW)

How can I handle discouragement?

1 Peter 5:8-9 *Watch out for attacks from the Devil. . . . Take a firm stand against him, and be strong in your faith. Remember that your Christian brothers and sisters all over the world are going through the same kind of suffering you are.*
When you are discouraged, you are particularly vulnerable to Satan's attacks. Be especially careful to stay close to God's Word and other believers during such difficult times.

1 Kings 19:10 *I alone am left, and now they are trying to kill me, too.*
Discouragement makes you feel sorry for yourself. Guard against thinking you are the only one who is going through troubles. It is encouraging to realize others are going through the same thing you are.

1 Samuel 1:10 *Hannah was in deep anguish, crying bitterly as she prayed to the LORD.*
Prayer is the first step you must take when discouraged, for it moves you into the presence of God.

2 Chronicles 20:15 *Don't be discouraged by this mighty army, for the battle is not yours, but God's.*
It would have been easy for the people of Judah to see only the vast enemy army and not see God standing by to destroy it. Discouragement can cause you to doubt God's love, drawing you away from the source of your greatest help.

How does God help me when I am discouraged?

Joshua 1:9 *I command you—be strong and courageous! Do not be afraid or discouraged. For the LORD your God is with you wherever you go.*
He helps by being with you.

John 15:18 *When the world hates you, remember it hated me before it hated you.*
He helps by understanding what you are going through.

Psalm 119:25, 28 *I lie in the dust, completely discouraged; revive me by your word. . . . I weep with grief; encourage me by your word.*
He helps by encouraging you through his Word.

Isaiah 40:29-31 *He gives power to those who are tired and worn out; he offers strength to the weak. Even youths will become exhausted, and young men will give up. But those who wait on the LORD will find new strength. They will fly high on wings like eagles. They will run and not grow weary. They will walk and not faint.*
He helps by giving you power and strength.

Psalm 40:2 *He lifted me out of the pit of despair, out of the mud and the mire. He set my feet on solid ground and steadied me as I walked along.*
He helps by rescuing and restoring you.

Joshua 23:10 *Each one of you will put to flight a thousand of the enemy, for the LORD your God fights for you, just as he has promised.*
He helps by defending you.

2 Thessalonians 2:16-17 *May our Lord Jesus Christ and God our Father, who loved us and in his special favor gave us everlasting comfort and good hope, comfort your hearts and give you strength in every good thing you do and say.*
He helps by comforting and strengthening you.

Psalm 138:3 *When I pray, you answer me; you encourage me by giving me the strength I need.*
He helps by answering your prayers.

1 Kings 19:5-6 *As he was sleeping, an angel touched him and told him, "Get up and eat!" He*

*looked around and saw some bread baked on hot
stones and a jar of water!*
He helps by meeting your needs.

2 Corinthians 7:6 *But God, who encourages
those who are discouraged, encouraged us by the
arrival of Titus.*
He helps by sending others to encourage you.

John 16:33 *I have told you all this so that you
may have peace in me. Here on earth you will have
many trials and sorrows. But take heart, because I
have overcome the world.*
He helps by flooding your soul with his peace.

How should I respond to feelings of discouragement?

Psalm 130:1 *From the depths of despair, O LORD,
I call for your help.*

1 Samuel 1:10 *Hannah was in deep anguish,
crying bitterly as she prayed to the LORD.*
Reach up to God in prayer, and he will lift you up.

James 4:10 *When you bow down before the Lord
and admit your dependence on him, he will lift you
up and give you honor.*
Acknowledge God's sovereignty and how much
you need his help.

Psalm 42:5-6 *Why am I discouraged? Why so
sad? I will put my hope in God! I will praise him
again—my Savior and my God! Now I am deeply
discouraged, but I will remember your kindness.*

When you remember who God is, then you can trust what he does and his promise to help you. Never separate yourself from the one who can give you the most help.

Psalm 55:22 *Give your burdens to the LORD, and he will take care of you. He will not permit the godly to slip and fall.*
Let God carry your burdens.

Psalm 142:3 *I am overwhelmed, and you alone know the way I should turn. Wherever I go, my enemies have set traps for me.*
Let God guide you when the way seems uncertain.

Zechariah 8:6 *This is what the LORD Almighty says: All this may seem impossible to you now, a small and discouraged remnant of God's people. But do you think this is impossible for me, the LORD Almighty?*
God can do the impossible, so let him!

1 Corinthians 15:58 *So, my dear brothers and sisters, be strong and steady, always enthusiastic about the Lord's work, for you know that nothing you do for the Lord is ever useless.*
Stir your enthusiasm for God's work, and then you will experience God's presence.

Hebrews 12:12 *Take a new grip with your tired hands and stand firm on your shaky legs.*
You must endure and never give up!

How can I help others who are feeling discouraged?

1 Samuel 23:16 *Jonathan went to find David and encouraged him to stay strong in his faith in God.* Encourage them in their relationship with God.

2 Chronicles 32:8 *"He may have a great army, but they are just men. We have the Lord our God to help us and to fight our battles for us!" These words greatly encouraged the people.* Remind them of what God can do and wants to do for and through them.

Titus 1:9 *He must have a strong and steadfast belief in the trustworthy message he was taught; then he will be able to encourage others with right teaching and show those who oppose it where they are wrong.* Share God's instruction and teaching with them.

Isaiah 35:3 *With this news, strengthen those who have tired hands, and encourage those who have weak knees.* Encourage them with hope for the future.

Jeremiah 8:21 *I weep for the hurt of my people. I am stunned and silent, mute with grief.*

Romans 12:15 *When others are happy, be happy with them. If they are sad, share their sorrow.* Be kind and empathetic to them.

PROMISE FROM GOD Revelation 21:4 *He will remove all of their sorrows, and there will be no more death or sorrow or crying or pain.*

Doubt

(*see also* FAITH)

Is it a sin to doubt God?

P s a l m   9 4 : 1 9   *When doubts filled my mind, your comfort gave me renewed hope and cheer.*
David and Thomas—along with many other saints—struggled with doubt. God doesn't mind doubt as long as you are seeking him in the midst of it. Doubt is sin if it leads you from God or if you allow it to turn to skepticism, then to cynicism, then to hardheartedness. But doubt can also become honest searching and lead you to reaffirm your faith in God.

What should I do when I find myself doubting?

H a b a k k u k   1 : 2   *How long, O LORD, must I call for help?*
Bring your doubts directly to God in prayer. Be candid and passionate as you pour out your heart to the Lord. Then even doubt can draw you closer to him.

M a r k   9 : 2 4   *The father instantly replied, "I do believe, but help me not to doubt!"*
Pray that God will give you the fullness of faith that you need.

Deuteronomy 7:18 *Don't be afraid of them! Just remember what the LORD your God did to Pharaoh and to all the land of Egypt.*

Mark 8:17-19 *Why are you so worried about having no food? . . . Don't you remember anything at all? What about the five thousand men I fed with five loaves of bread?*
When you are struggling with experiential doubt, take time to remember the way God has worked in the Bible and in your life. Then you will grow confident that he is real and will work in your present situation.

John 20:27 *Then he said to Thomas, "Put your finger here and see my hands. Put your hand into the wound in my side."*
When you have intellectual doubts, check out the evidence.

Habakkuk 2:1 *I will climb up into my watch-tower now and wait to see what the LORD will say to me and how he will answer my complaint.*
Be patient. Let God answer your questions on his schedule, not yours. Don't throw away your faith just because God doesn't resolve your doubt immediately.

1 Thessalonians 5:11 *Encourage each other and build each other up, just as you are already doing.*

Hebrews 10:25 *Let us not neglect our meeting together.*
When you are wrestling with doubt, keep attending church and stay close to other Christians. Resist the temptation to isolate yourself, for that will only serve to weaken your faith more. Doubt feeds on loneliness.

PROMISE FROM GOD Hebrews 13:5 *For God has said, "I will never fail you. I will never forsake you."*

Emotions

During these troubled times, I feel so emotional. Is it okay to be open with my emotions?

Ezra 3:12 *Many of the older priests, Levites, and other leaders remembered the first Temple, and they wept aloud when they saw the new Temple's foundation. The others, however, were shouting for joy.*

2 Samuel 18:33 *The king was overcome with emotion. He went up to his room over the gateway and burst into tears. And as he went, he cried, "O my son Absalom! My son, my son Absalom! If only I could have died instead of you! O Absalom, my son, my son."*
It is not a sign of weakness to display your emotions. It is, rather, a sign of your humanity

and an important component of your emotional health.

Job 7:11 *I cannot keep from speaking. I must express my anguish. I must complain in my bitterness.* Keep an open dialogue with the Lord and others you trust so you are not covering up your emotions.

Matthew 26:38 *He told them, "My soul is crushed with grief to the point of death. Stay here and watch with me."* Jesus was honest with his disciples about his deep emotions. You also need this openness with trusted friends.

PROMISE FROM GOD Galatians 5:22-23 *But when the Holy Spirit controls our lives, he will produce this kind of fruit in us: love, joy, peace, patience, kindness, goodness, faithfulness, gentleness, and self-control.*

Empathy

What is empathy?

2 Corinthians 11:28-29 *Then, besides all this, I have the daily burden of how the churches are getting along. Who is weak without my feeling that weakness? Who is led astray, and I do not burn with anger?*

Empathy is deeply identifying with another's pain or position and responding with a desire to bring comfort.

How is God empathetic toward me?

Isaiah 63:9 *In all their suffering he also suffered, and he personally rescued them. In his love and mercy he redeemed them. He lifted them up and carried them through all the years.*

Hebrews 5:2 *And because he is human, he is able to deal gently with the people, though they are ignorant and wayward. For he is subject to the same weaknesses they have.*

Because God the Father loved us, he planned to rescue us from the pain and eternal consequences of sin. Jesus successfully accomplished this through his life, death, and resurrection. Because Jesus came to earth as a human being, he can empathize with us. He understands our weaknesses and our fears. Both Jesus and the Holy Spirit plead for you today that you would be free from the hurt that comes from sin and experience the joy and freedom of a relationship with the eternal God.

How can I be more empathetic toward others?

2 Corinthians 1:3-4 *All praise to the God and Father of our Lord Jesus Christ. He is the source*

*of every mercy and the God who comforts us. He
comforts us in all our troubles so that we can comfort
others. When others are troubled, we will be able
to give them the same comfort God has given us.*
You can rely on God, the source of all mercy
and comfort, as you minister to others.

Galatians 6:2 *Share each other's troubles and
problems, and in this way obey the law of Christ.*

1 Corinthians 12:26 *If one part suffers, all
the parts suffer with it, and if one part is honored,
all the parts are glad.*
You should be more than merely concerned
about others' troubles and problems. To be
empathetic, you need to be emotionally involved
in other people's lives, sharing their troubles and
problems.

Luke 6:31 *Do for others as you would like them
to do for you.*
You can minister in ways you would like to be
ministered to in similar circumstances. When
you don't know what to do, ask yourself what
you would want someone to do for you in that
situation.

PROMISE FROM GOD Romans
12:15 *When others are happy, be happy with them.
If they are sad, share their sorrow.*

Encouragement

How does God encourage me?

1 Kings 19:4-6 *Then he went on alone into the desert, traveling all day. He sat down under a solitary broom tree and prayed that he might die. "I have had enough, LORD," he said. . . . But as he was sleeping, an angel touched him and told him, "Get up and eat!" He looked around and saw some bread baked on hot stones and a jar of water!*
He meets your needs at just the right time.

Psalm 138:3 *When I pray, you answer me; you encourage me by giving me the strength I need.*
He gives you strength when you ask.

Psalm 119:25,28 *I lie in the dust, completely discouraged; revive me by your word. I weep with grief; encourage me by your word.*

Romans 15:4 *Such things were written in the Scriptures long ago to teach us. They give us hope and encouragement as we wait patiently for God's promises.*
He's given his written Word to revive you and offer you hope.

Matthew 9:2 *Some people brought to him a paralyzed man on a mat. Seeing their faith, Jesus said to the paralyzed man, "Take heart, son! Your sins are forgiven."*
He forgives your sins.

How can I be an encouragement to others?

1 Samuel 23:16 *Jonathan went to find David and encouraged him to stay strong in his faith in God.*
By helping them keep a close relationship with God.

Ephesians 4:29 *Don't use foul or abusive language. Let everything you say be good and helpful, so that your words will be an encouragement to those who hear them.*
By making sure everything you say is kind and uplifting.

2 Chronicles 30:22 *Hezekiah encouraged the Levites for the skill they displayed as they served the LORD.*
By complimenting them for a job well done.

Titus 1:9 *He must have a strong and steadfast belief in the trustworthy message he was taught; then he will be able to encourage others with right teaching and show those who oppose it where they are wrong.*
By sharing God's instruction and correction.

Proverbs 15:30 *A cheerful look brings joy to the heart; good news makes for good health.*
By a smile!

PROMISE FROM GOD 2 Thessalonians 2:16-17 *May our Lord Jesus Christ and God our Father . . . comfort your hearts and give you strength in every good thing you do and say.*

Endurance

In what areas should I develop endurance?

Deuteronomy 12:1 *These are the laws and regulations you must obey as long as you live in the land the LORD, the God of your ancestors, is giving you.*
In obedience. You must consistently obey God, not just obey him once in a while. Sometimes that will take endurance because obedience isn't always easy.

Psalm 119:147-148 *I rise early, before the sun is up; I cry out for help and put my hope in your words. I stay awake through the night, thinking about your promise.*

Psalm 17:5 *My steps have stayed on your path; I have not wavered from following you.*
In seeking, believing, and faithfully following God. Endurance shows that your faith and your conversion are real, having a lasting impact on your life.

1 Corinthians 4:12 *We have worked wearily with our own hands to earn our living. We bless those who curse us. We are patient with those who abuse us.*
In dealing with difficult people. You must endure with kindness and patience as you deal with people who make life tough on you. This is the only way to win them over, by patiently pouring on them the love of Christ.

2 Thessalonians 1:4 *We proudly tell God's other churches about your endurance and faithfulness in all the persecutions and hardships you are suffering.*

Acts 14:22 *They encouraged them to continue in the faith, reminding them that they must enter into the Kingdom of God through many tribulations.*
In suffering through persecutions, hardships, trials, and tribulations. Endurance through such times demonstrates that your faith is strong and real and can withstand any difficult test.

Galatians 6:9 *So don't get tired of doing what is good. Don't get discouraged and give up, for we will reap a harvest of blessing at the appropriate time.*
In doing good. It is difficult to do good over a long period of time when life throws you so many trials and temptations. An enduring faith, however, is up to the challenge.

How do I develop endurance?

Romans 15:5 *May God, who gives this patience and encouragement, help you live in complete harmony with each other—each with the attitude of Christ Jesus toward the other.*

Ephesians 6:13 *Use every piece of God's armor to resist the enemy in the time of evil, so that after the battle you will still be standing firm.*
Endurance originates with God. He is your source of the power and perseverance you need to endure.

Hebrews 12:2-3 *We do this by keeping our eyes on Jesus, on whom our faith depends from start to finish. He was willing to die a shameful death on the cross because of the joy he knew would be his afterward. . . . Think about all he endured when sinful people did such terrible things to him, so that you don't become weary and give up.*

The next time you are tempted to give up, think of Jesus on the cross.

Romans 5:3 *We can rejoice, too, when we run into problems and trials, for we know that they are good for us—they help us learn to endure.*

Of course you don't like problems, trials, troubles, and the testing of your faith, for they can drag you down. But they can also lift you up, and when they do, you have learned endurance.

Habakkuk 2:3 *But these things I plan won't happen right away. Slowly, steadily, surely, the time approaches when the vision will be fulfilled. If it seems slow, wait patiently, for it will surely take place. It will not be delayed.*

You develop endurance by maintaining an eternal perspective inspired by hope.

PROMISE FROM GOD James 1:2-4 *Dear brothers and sisters, whenever trouble comes your way, let it be an opportunity for joy. For when your faith is tested, your endurance has a chance to grow. So let it grow, for when your endurance is fully* *developed, you will be strong in character and ready for anything.*

Enemies

As Christians, we know there are many people who consider themselves our enemies. How do those enemies try to hurt us?

Numbers 25:16-18 *Then the LORD said to Moses, "Attack the Midianites and destroy them, because they assaulted you with deceit by tricking you into worshiping Baal of Peor."*
By trying to lead believers into sin.

2 Chronicles 32:10, 15 *"This is what King Sennacherib of Assyria says: What are you trusting in that makes you think you can survive my siege of Jerusalem? Don't let Hezekiah fool you! Don't let him deceive you like this! I say it again—no god of any nation has ever yet been able to rescue his people from me or my ancestors. How much less will your God rescue you from my power!"*
By trying to confuse and divide us.

Ezra 4:1-3 *The enemies of Judah and Benjamin heard that the exiles were rebuilding a Temple to the LORD, the God of Israel. So they approached Zerubbabel and the other leaders and said, "Let us build with you, for we worship your God just as you do. We have sacrificed to him ever since King Esarhaddon of*

*Assyria brought us here." But Zerubbabel, Jeshua, and
the other leaders of Israel replied, "You may have no
part in this work, for we have nothing in common."*
By trying to get us to compromise in our faith
and beliefs.

Joshua 17:16 *They said, "The hill country is not
enough for us, and the Canaanites in the lowlands
around Beth-shan and the valley of Jezreel have iron
chariots—they are too strong for us."*
By trying to intimidate us.

Judges 16:5 *The leaders of the Philistines went
to her and said, "Find out from Samson what makes
him so strong and how he can be overpowered and
tied up securely. Then each of us will give you eleven
hundred pieces of silver."*
By finding our vulnerability and trying to use
it against us.

Lamentations 1:7 *And now in the midst of
her sadness and wandering, Jerusalem remembers
her ancient splendor. But then she fell to her enemy,
and there was no one to help her. Her enemy struck
her down and laughed as she fell.*
By using aggression and humiliation. When we
seem to be defeated, they rejoice. That's when we
need to hold on to our faith and pray for God to
work all things together for his good and for his
glory.

Where can I turn when I feel overwhelmed by those who are working against me—my enemies?

Psalm 71:1-2 *O LORD, you are my refuge; never let me be disgraced. Rescue me! Save me from my enemies, for you are just.*

Psalm 140:1-2 *O LORD, rescue me from evil people. Preserve me from those who are violent, those who plot evil in their hearts and stir up trouble all day long.*

Turn to God and not away from him, for he is the only one who can really help you.

Deuteronomy 33:27 *The eternal God is your refuge, and his everlasting arms are under you. He thrusts out the enemy before you; it is he who cries, "Destroy them!"*

Psalm 91:1-4 *Those who live in the shelter of the Most High will find rest in the shadow of the Almighty. This I declare of the LORD: He alone is my refuge, my place of safety; he is my God, and I am trusting him. For he will rescue you from every trap and protect you from the fatal plague. He will shield you with his wings. He will shelter you with his feathers. His faithful promises are your armor and protection.*

Seek God's protection. He is strong when you are weak. He is your place of safety when you are vulnerable and under attack.

Psalm 5:8 *Lead me in the right path, O LORD, or my enemies will conquer me. Tell me clearly what to do, and show me which way to turn.*

2 Samuel 5:17-19 *When the Philistines heard that David had been anointed king of Israel, they mobilized all their forces to capture him. But David was told they were coming and went into the stronghold. The Philistines arrived and spread out across the valley of Rephaim. So David asked the LORD, "Should I go out to fight the Philistines? Will you hand them over to me?" The LORD replied, "Yes, go ahead. I will certainly give you the victory."*

Follow God's direction and instructions. You will run out of options, but he is the God of unlimited resources. Only he can show you the way to victory.

Joshua 6:2-5 *But the LORD said to Joshua, "I have given you Jericho, its king, and all its mighty warriors. Your entire army is to march around the city once a day for six days. Seven priests will walk ahead of the Ark, each carrying a ram's horn. On the seventh day you are to march around the city seven times, with the priests blowing the horns. When you hear the priests give one long blast on the horns, have all the people give a mighty shout. Then the walls of the city will collapse, and the people can charge straight into the city."*

Respond in obedience to God. If you don't follow his instructions, you will not know how to be victorious.

2 Samuel 22:40 *You have armed me with strength for the battle; you have subdued my enemies under my feet.*

Ezra 8:31 *We broke camp at the Ahava Canal on April 19 and started off to Jerusalem. And the gracious hand of our God protected us and saved us from enemies and bandits along the way.*
Trust God for the outcome. Evil cannot defeat God, so if you are on his side, victory is sure.

How should I respond to my enemies?

Matthew 5:43-45 *You have heard that the law of Moses says, "Love your neighbor" and hate your enemy. But I say, love your enemies! Pray for those who persecute you! In that way, you will be acting as true children of your Father in heaven.*

Proverbs 25:21-22 *If your enemies are hungry, give them food to eat. If they are thirsty, give them water to drink. You will heap burning coals on their heads, and the LORD will reward you.*

Proverbs 24:17-18 *Do not rejoice when your enemies fall into trouble. Don't be happy when they stumble. For the LORD will be displeased with you and will turn his anger away from them.*

Romans 12:19 *Dear friends, never avenge yourselves. Leave that to God. For it is written, "I will take vengeance; I will repay those who deserve it," says the Lord.*

Respond to your enemies—no matter what they try to do—with loving forgiveness. Your actions toward your enemies should include prayer for them as well as acts of kindness. Your words should be gentle. Your attitude should not be one of revenge or ill will. This is what Jesus would do; this is what sets you apart from the rest of the world. When you act this way, the world will take notice.

PROMISE FROM GOD Deuteronomy 20:1 *When you go out to fight your enemies and you face horses and chariots and an army greater than your own, do not be afraid. The LORD your God, who brought you safely out of Egypt, is with you!*

Evil

Why does evil exist?
Daniel 7:25 *He will defy the Most High and wear down the holy people of the Most High.* The purpose of evil is to wear down believers until they are led into sin. This gives Satan pleasure and greater power over the earth.

If God is good, why does he let evil continue to exist and let people do evil things?
Genesis 2:15-17 *The LORD God placed the man in the Garden of Eden to tend and care for it.*

But the LORD God gave him this warning: "You may freely eat any fruit in the garden except fruit from the tree of the knowledge of good and evil. If you eat of its fruit, you will surely die."

Genuine love requires the freedom to choose. From the beginning, God desired a loving relationship with humans, so he gave us this freedom. But with the ability to make choices comes the possibility of choosing our own way over God's way. Our own way always leads to sin. This breaks God's heart, but the alternative would have been to make us robots, not humans. Evil still exists and evil people continue to do evil things, but we can choose to do right. And when we do so, God is greatly pleased.

Where does evil come from?

Jeremiah 17:9 *The human heart is most deceitful and desperately wicked. Who really knows how bad it is?*

Our own hearts, polluted by sin and selfishness, are the source of much that is evil.

Ephesians 6:12 *For we are not fighting against people made of flesh and blood, but against the evil rulers and authorities of the unseen world, against those mighty powers of darkness who rule this world, and against wicked spirits in the heavenly realms.*

Cosmic forces of evil, led by Satan, are engaged in a deadly rebellion against God.

How can I combat evil?

Romans 12:9 *Hate what is wrong. Stand on the side of good.*
Resolve to hate everything that is sinful and evil.

Romans 13:14 *But let the Lord Jesus Christ take control of you, and don't think of ways to indulge your evil desires.*
Surrender yourself to Christ's control. Make sure that you don't put yourself in situations where you know your resolve for righteousness will be tested. The closer you walk with Christ, the harder it is to be caught in the snare of evil.

Ephesians 6:10-11 *A final word: Be strong with the Lord's mighty power. Put on all of God's armor so that you will be able to stand firm against all strategies and tricks of the Devil.*
Realize that your own strength is insufficient to combat evil. With God's strength and protection, however, you can win any battle.

Romans 12:21 *Don't let evil get the best of you, but conquer evil by doing good.*
Combat evil with good. It is one of the most difficult things to do, but ultimately, it is the only thing that will work.

It often seems that evil is winning. Can this really be?

John 16:33 *Here on earth you will have many*

*trials and sorrows. But take heart, because I have
overcome the world.*

It will appear at times that evil has the upper
hand, but the Lord's power is supreme and he
will win the final victory.

Revelation 21:4 *He will remove all of their
sorrows, and there will be no more death or sorrow
or crying or pain. For the old world and its evils are
gone forever.*

When Jesus returns to usher in eternity, he will
eradicate evil forever. No matter how bleak things
may seem now, we are on the winning side!

Why do people often seem to get away with evil?

Jeremiah 12:1-2 *Why are the wicked so
prosperous? Why are evil people so happy? You have
planted them, and they have taken root and prospered.
Your name is on their lips, but in their hearts they give
you no credit at all.*

Psalm 73:17-20 *One day I went into your
sanctuary, O God, and I thought about the destiny
of the wicked. Truly, you put them on a slippery path
and send them sliding over the cliff to destruction. In
an instant they are destroyed, swept away by terrors.
Their present life is only a dream that is gone when
they awake.*

Many have struggled with the fact that not only
does evil often go unpunished on this earth, but

evildoers actually seem to get ahead! However, one day all of us will stand before God's judgment seat. The present prosperity of evildoers is only temporary. This present life lasts only for a moment; eternity is forever.

Isaiah 32:7-8 *The smooth tricks of evil people will be exposed, including all the lies they use to oppress the poor in the courts. But good people will be generous to others and will be blessed for all they do.* It seems that people today can do anything they want and not only get away with it, but flourish. God has promised, however, that in his time everyone will be judged, evil will be exposed, and the righteous will prevail. If righteousness always prevailed on earth, then people wouldn't follow God for the right reasons—they would follow God only to have an easy life. God doesn't promise the absence of evil on this earth. In fact, he guarantees that evil will be pervasive and powerful. But God promises to help us stand against evil, and if we do, we will receive our reward of eternal life with him in heaven, where evil will be no more.

PROMISE FROM GOD Revelation 20:10 *Then the Devil, who betrayed them, was thrown into the lake of fire that burns with sulfur, joining the beast and the false prophet. There they will be tormented day and night forever and ever.*

Faith

Why should I have faith in God?

John 5:24 I assure you, those who listen to my message and believe in God who sent me have eternal life.

Faith is the only way to get to heaven. It is the only doorway to eternal life. If God created eternity, then only through God can you get there.

Hebrews 11:1 What is faith? It is the confident assurance that what we hope for is going to happen.

Faith gives us hope. When the world seems to be a crazy, mixed-up place, believers can rest in the fact that one day God will come and make it all right. Our faith in his promise to do that some-day allows us to keep going today.

How can I strengthen my faith?

Genesis 12:1, 4 The LORD told Abram, "Leave your country. . . ." So Abram departed as the LORD had instructed him.

Like a muscle, faith gets stronger the more you exercise it. When you follow God and see him come through for you, your faith will be stronger when you encounter the next trial or test.

Psalm 119:48, 54 I honor and love your commands. I meditate on your principles. . . . Your principles have been the music of my life throughout the years of my pilgrimage.

Your faith will grow stronger as you study the Bible and reflect on the truths it sets forth about who God is and his guidelines for your life.

When I'm struggling in my Christian life and have doubts, does it mean I have less faith?

Genesis 15:8 *But Abram replied, "O Sovereign LORD, how can I be sure that you will give it to me?"*

Matthew 11:2-3 *John the Baptist . . . sent his disciples to ask Jesus, "Are you really the Messiah we've been waiting for?"*

Many people in the Bible whom we consider to be "pillars of faith" had moments of doubt. The key is to bring your doubts directly to the Lord. Doubts are valuable when they bring you closer to God.

PROMISE FROM GOD 2 Thessalonians 1:10 *You will be among those praising him on that day, for you believed what we testified about him.*

Faithfulness

Is God faithful?

Psalm 89:5 *All heaven will praise your miracles, LORD; myriads of angels will praise you for your faithfulness.*

Deuteronomy 7:9 *He is the faithful God who keeps his covenant for a thousand generations.*

2 Thessalonians 3:3 *But the Lord is faithful; he will make you strong and guard you from the evil one.*

God is completely faithful. His faithfulness is so great it makes the angels sing!

In what ways does God show his faithfulness to me?

Luke 1:68-70 *Praise the Lord, the God of Israel, because he has visited his people and redeemed them. He has sent us a mighty Savior from the royal line of his servant David, just as he promised through his holy prophets long ago.*

God has faithfully fulfilled his promise to send a Savior.

Psalm 4:3 *The LORD will answer when I call to him.*

Psalm 143:1 *Hear my prayer, O LORD; listen to my plea! Answer me because you are faithful and righteous.*

When you call on God, he faithfully answers.

1 Corinthians 1:9 *God . . . always does just what he says, and he is the one who invited you into this wonderful friendship with his Son, Jesus Christ our Lord.*

God faithfully does what he says he will do. As you read the Bible, you will discover myriads of promises that have already been fulfilled. Now when you read the promises yet to come, you can count on God's faithfulness to fulfill them because he always does just what he says.

PROMISE FROM GOD Deuteronomy 32:4 *He is the Rock; his work is perfect. Everything he does is just and fair. He is a faithful God who does no wrong; how just and upright he is!*

Farewells

What will help me say good-bye in a healthy and positive way?

Acts 20:36-38 *When he had finished speaking, he knelt and prayed with them. They wept aloud as they embraced him in farewell, sad most of all because he had said that they would never see him again.* Praying together and being open and honest about the pain of parting are important to healthy good-byes.

Philemon 7 *I myself have gained much joy and comfort from your love, my brother, because your kindness has so often refreshed the hearts of God's people.* It is essential to take time before parting to thank people for what they have meant to you.

Genesis 12:4 *So Abram departed as the LORD had instructed him.*

Seeing God's hand in your circumstances and following God's call in your life will give you greater security as you say good-bye, even though parting will still not be easy.

Psalm 139:9-10 *If I ride the wings of the morning, if I dwell by the farthest oceans, even there your hand will guide me, and your strength will support me.*
Never stop reminding yourself that God is the constant in your life and that he is enough. No matter where you have to go, even across the "farthest oceans," God's hand will guide you and give you strength for the task ahead.

Acts 20:32 *And now I entrust you to God and the word of his grace—his message that is able to build you up and give you an inheritance with all those he has set apart for himself.*
There is great comfort in knowing that God will take care of those to whom you say farewell.

2 Timothy 4:7 *I have fought a good fight, I have finished the race, and I have remained faithful.*
Parting is easier if you have lived in such a way as to minimize regrets and unfinished business.

How should I bid others farewell? What can make a farewell easier?

Ruth 1:8-9 *But on the way, Naomi said to her two daughters-in-law, "Go back to your mothers' homes instead of coming with me. And may the LORD reward you for your kindness to your husbands and to me. May the LORD bless you with the security of another marriage."*

Putting the other person's needs ahead of your own needs.

1 Samuel 20:42 *At last Jonathan said to David, "Go in peace, for we have made a pact in the LORD's name. We have entrusted each other and each other's children into the LORD's hands forever." Then David left, and Jonathan returned to the city.*

Entrusting the other person into God's care while you are gone.

Genesis 24:58-60 *So they called Rebekah. "Are you willing to go with this man?" they asked her. And she replied, "Yes, I will go." So they said good-bye to Rebekah and sent her away with Abraham's servant and his men. . . . They blessed her with this blessing as she parted: "Our sister, may you become the mother of many millions! May your descendants overcome all their enemies."*

Don't hold on. Allow the departure—with a blessing!

2 Timothy 1:4 *I long to see you again, for I remember your tears as we parted. And I will be filled with joy when we are together again.*

Anticipate the next meeting.

What should be my perspective on farewells caused by death?

Ecclesiastes 8:8 *None of us can hold back our spirit from departing.*
Realize that death is inevitable.

Isaiah 25:8 *He will swallow up death forever! The Sovereign LORD will wipe away all tears. He will remove forever all insults and mockery against his land and people. The LORD has spoken!*
Realize God's ultimate power over death.

Matthew 25:46 *They will go away into eternal punishment, but the righteous will go into eternal life.*
Realize that there is life after death.

Revelation 7:17 *The Lamb who stands in front of the throne will be their Shepherd. He will lead them to the springs of life-giving water. And God will wipe away all their tears.*
Realize the eternal quality of life after death for the Christian.

PROMISE FROM GOD Matthew 28:20 *And be sure of this: I am with you always, even to the end of the age.*

Fear

These are frightening times. What can I do when I am overcome with fear?
Psalm 46:1-2 *God is our refuge and strength, always ready to help in times of trouble. So we will*

not fear, even if earthquakes come and the mountains crumble into the sea.

Deuteronomy 31:6 *Be strong and courageous! Do not be afraid of them! The LORD your God will go ahead of you. He will neither fail you nor forsake you.*
Remind yourself that God is always with you. The situation in the world may be genuinely threatening—and you may have reason to be afraid—but remember that God has not abandoned you and he promises to stay with you. Even if your situation is so bad that it ends up causing your death, God will not have left you, but will have ushered you into his very presence instead.

Ephesians 1:3 *How we praise God, the Father of our Lord Jesus Christ, who has blessed us with every spiritual blessing in the heavenly realms.*
Remind yourself that no enemy or adversity can take away your most important blessings: your forgiveness, your relationship with God, and your eternal salvation. These remain secure in Christ even when the world seems to be falling apart.

Revelation 22:5 *The Lord God will shine on them. And they will reign forever and ever.*
Remind yourself that as a Christian, your destiny is victory! The troubles of this world are only temporary. You can go forward with the confidence that you are on the winning side.

Philippians 4:6-7 *Don't worry about anything; instead, pray about everything. Tell God what you need, and thank him for all he has done. If you do this, you will experience God's peace, which is far more wonderful than the human mind can understand. His peace will guard your hearts and minds as you live in Christ Jesus.*

Pray with a thankful heart, asking God to give you what you need to deal with your fears. Peace is not the absence of fear, but the conquest of fear. Peace is not running away, but overcoming. Ask God to give you his peace that passes understanding.

PROMISE FROM GOD Isaiah 41:10 *Don't be afraid, for I am with you. Do not be dismayed, for I am your God. I will strengthen you. I will help you. I will uphold you with my victorious right hand.*

Forgiveness

I think I need to make things right with God, but I don't understand his forgiveness. What does it really mean to be forgiven?

Colossians 1:22 *You are holy and blameless as you stand before him without a single fault.*

Isaiah 1:18 *No matter how deep the stain of your sins, I can remove it. I can make you as clean as freshly fallen snow.*

Forgiveness means that God looks at you as though you have never sinned. You are completely blameless before him.

A c t s 8 : 2 2 - 2 3 *Perhaps he will forgive your evil thoughts, for I can see that you are . . . held captive by sin.*
Forgiveness frees you from slavery to sin.

M a t t h e w 5 : 4 4 *Love your enemies! Pray for those who persecute you!*
Forgiveness paves the way for harmonious relationships, even with your enemies.

R o m a n s 4 : 7 *Oh, what joy for those whose disobedience is forgiven, whose sins are put out of sight.*
Forgiveness brings great joy.

I've done some pretty awful things. How can God forgive me?

P s a l m 5 1 : 4 *Against you, and you alone, have I sinned; I have done what is evil in your sight.*
God will forgive when you admit that you have sinned against him—that you have done wrong in his eyes.

1 J o h n 1 : 8 - 9 *If we say we have no sin, we are only fooling ourselves and refusing to accept the truth. But if we confess our sins to him, he is faithful and just to forgive us and to cleanse us from every wrong.*
You will receive God's forgiveness when you confess your sins to him, stop doing what is wrong, and turn to him with all your heart.

Matthew 26:28 *This is my blood, which seals the covenant between God and his people. It is poured out to forgive the sins of many.*
Jesus died so that God's forgiveness would be freely available to you. Jesus took the punishment your sins deserved.

Acts 10:43 *Everyone who believes in him will have their sins forgiven through his name.*

Acts 13:38 *In this man Jesus there is forgiveness for your sins.*
You receive God's forgiveness by trusting in Christ as your Savior and Lord. All you need to do is ask him.

How can I forgive someone who has hurt me very badly?

Ephesians 4:31 *Get rid of all bitterness, rage, anger, harsh words, and slander, as well as all types of malicious behavior.*
Remember that unforgiveness not only ruins your relationships, it also poisons your soul. The person most hurt by unforgiveness is you.

Ephesians 4:32 *Instead, be kind to one another, forgiving each other, just as God through Christ has forgiven you.*
God's forgiveness through Christ's death is the motivation and the model for your forgiveness of others. If God has forgiven you, how can you refuse to forgive someone who has wronged you?

And your forgiveness, like God's, is a gift of grace, free to the recipient yet costly to the giver.

Romans 12:19 *Dear friends, never avenge yourselves. Leave that to God. For it is written, "I will take vengeance; I will repay those who deserve it," says the Lord.*
Punishing evildoers is God's job, not yours, and God can be trusted to do his job. Therefore, you can remove yourself from the endless cycle of revenge and retaliation by forgiving.

PROMISE FROM GOD Luke 24:47 *With my authority, take this message of repentance to all the nations, beginning in Jerusalem: "There is forgiveness of sins for all who turn to me."*

Future

How can I face the future when it is so uncertain?
Hebrews 13:8 *Jesus Christ is the same yesterday, today, and forever.*

Psalm 121:8 *The LORD keeps watch over you as you come and go, both now and forever.*
You can face the uncertain future because you have an unchanging God who loves and guides you. As the old saying puts it: We know not what the future holds, but we know who holds the future.

John 16:33 *Here on earth you will have many trials and sorrows. But take heart, because I have overcome the world.*
Jesus never promised a problem free life; in fact, he promised just the opposite. So don't be surprised or fearful in hard times. Jesus is greater than any problem you will ever encounter.

Matthew 6:34 *So don't worry about tomorrow, for tomorrow will bring its own worries. Today's trouble is enough for today.*
Most of the things we worry might happen never do. So don't waste time on the "what if" worries. Spend your worry time as prayer time.

What are some promises I can look forward to in my future with God?

1 John 3:2 *Yes, dear friends, we are already God's children, and we can't even imagine what we will be like when Christ returns. But we do know that when he comes we will be like him, for we will see him as he really is.*
You will one day be like Christ.

Jeremiah 29:11 *"I know the plans I have for you," says the LORD. "They are plans for good and not for disaster, to give you a future and a hope."*
The great plans God has for you will someday be revealed and fulfilled. Spend today knowing God better. Then, tomorrow, you will better know his plans for you.

John 14:1-4 *Don't be troubled. You trust God, now trust in me. There are many rooms in my Father's home, and I am going to prepare a place for you. If this were not so, I would tell you plainly. When everything is ready, I will come and get you, so that you will always be with me where I am. And you know where I am going and how to get there.* When you die, you will go to live with Christ in his home forever.

1 Peter 1:4-5 *God has reserved a priceless inheritance for his children. It is kept in heaven for you, pure and undefiled, beyond the reach of change and decay. And God, in his mighty power, will protect you until you receive this salvation, because you are trusting him. It will be revealed on the last day for all to see.* You will inherit the heavenly riches reserved for God's children.

Revelation 3:5 *All who are victorious will be clothed in white. I will never erase their names from the Book of Life, but I will announce before my Father and his angels that they are mine.* You will wear the garments of heaven and be identified with Christ.

Revelation 21:4 *He will remove all of their sorrows, and there will be no more death or sorrow or crying or pain. For the old world and its evils are gone forever.*

In heaven you will never hurt, cry, have pain, or experience sorrow. Evil will be gone forever.

Colossians 3:4 *When Christ, who is your real life, is revealed to the whole world, you will share in all his glory.*
You will share the glory that belongs to Christ.

1 Corinthians 15:24 *After that the end will come, when he will turn the Kingdom over to God the Father, having put down all enemies of every kind.*

Revelation 11:15 *Then the seventh angel blew his trumpet, and there were loud voices shouting in heaven: "The whole world has now become the kingdom of our Lord and of his Christ, and he will reign forever and ever."*

Zechariah 14:9 *And the LORD will be king over all the earth. On that day there will be one LORD— his name alone will be worshiped.*
You will be part of an eternal kingdom ruled by the Lord God himself. It will be free from God's enemies.

1 Thessalonians 4:17 *Then, together with them, we who are still alive and remain on the earth will be caught up in the clouds to meet the Lord in the air and remain with him forever.*
When you die, you will live forever with Christ in heaven.

Matthew 26:64 *Jesus replied, "Yes, it is as you say. And in the future you will see me, the Son of*

Man, sitting at God's right hand in the place of power and coming back on the clouds of heaven."

Acts 1:11 *They said, "Men of Galilee, why are you standing here staring at the sky? Jesus has been taken away from you into heaven. And someday, just as you saw him go, he will return!"*
Someday in the future you will see Christ return again to earth.

1 Corinthians 15:52 *It will happen in a moment, in the blinking of an eye, when the last trumpet is blown. For when the trumpet sounds, the Christians who have died will be raised with transformed bodies. And then we who are living will be transformed so that we will never die.*
When Christ returns again to earth, he will raise up Christians with transformed bodies that will never die.

2 Thessalonians 2:8 *Then the man of lawlessness will be revealed, whom the Lord Jesus will consume with the breath of his mouth and destroy by the splendor of his coming.*

Hebrews 2:14 *Because God's children are human beings—made of flesh and blood—Jesus also became flesh and blood by being born in human form. For only as a human being could he die, and only by dying could he break the power of the Devil, who had the power of death.*
Christ will break the power of death and of Satan.

How can these promises about the future help me live today?

2 Corinthians 4:17 *Our present troubles are quite small and won't last very long. Yet they produce for us an immeasurably great glory that will last forever!* As a heaven-bound follower of Jesus, you need to put heaven and earth in perspective. The years we spend living on earth now appear miniscule in comparison to the endless ages we will spend with God in his heavenly kingdom. This eternal perspective helps you to live here on earth with the right priorities, for this life is really your preparation for life in heaven.

PROMISE FROM GOD 1 Corinthians 2:9 *That is what the Scriptures mean when they say, "No eye has seen, no ear has heard, and no mind has imagined what God has prepared for those who love him."*

Grief

Something terrible has happened, Lord. I need you to minister to me. How will you do that?

Psalm 10:14 *But you do see the trouble and grief they cause. You take note of it and punish them. The helpless put their trust in you. You are the defender of orphans.*

God ministers to you through his personal attention.

Psalm 23:4 *Even when I walk through the dark valley of death, I will not be afraid, for you are close beside me. Your rod and your staff protect and comfort me.*

God ministers to you through his comforting presence.

Psalm 119:28, 50, 52, 92 *I weep with grief; encourage me by your word. . . . Your promise revives me; it comforts me in all my troubles. . . . I meditate on your age-old laws; O LORD, they comfort me. . . . If your law hadn't sustained me with joy, I would have died in my misery.*

God ministers to you through his Word.

Romans 8:26-27 *And the Holy Spirit helps us in our distress. For we don't even know what we should pray for, nor how we should pray. But the Holy Spirit prays for us with groanings that cannot be expressed in words. And the Father who knows all hearts knows what the Spirit is saying, for the Spirit pleads for us believers in harmony with God's own will.*

God ministers to you through his Spirit. When you don't even know what to pray, the Holy Spirit will pray for you.

John 16:20 *Truly, you will weep and mourn over what is going to happen to me, but the world will rejoice. You will grieve, but your grief will suddenly turn to wonderful joy when you see me again.*

God ministers to you through his ultimate plan for good. He weeps with you and he understands. He loves you and will walk through this dark valley with you. God will dry the tears of your mourning and bring a smile to your face. It may not seem that way today, but trust him. You will come out on the other side.

2 Corinthians 7:6 *But God, who encourages those who are discouraged, encouraged us by the arrival of Titus.*
God ministers to you through his gift of other people in your life. When you need encouragement, God will bring friends and counselors.

1 Thessalonians 4:13-14 *And now, brothers and sisters, I want you to know what will happen to the Christians who have died so you will not be full of sorrow like people who have no hope. For since we believe that Jesus died and was raised to life again, we also believe that when Jesus comes, God will bring back with Jesus all the Christians who have died.*
God ministers to you through his promise of eternity with him, free of all grief. When you lose perspective, ask God to show you a glimpse of eternity.

I want to believe that something positive can come of this. How can God use my grief for good?
2 Corinthians 7:10 *God can use sorrow in our*

lives to help us turn away from sin and seek salvation. We will never regret that kind of sorrow. But sorrow without repentance is the kind that results in death. Times of grief can lead to confession, repentance, and a restored relationship with God. When grief leaves your soul empty, God can fill it with more than you ever dreamed was possible.

Lamentations 3:18-25 *I cry out, "My splendor is gone! Everything I had hoped for from the LORD is lost!" The thought of my suffering and homelessness is bitter beyond words. I will never forget this awful time, as I grieve over my loss. Yet I still dare to hope when I remember this: The unfailing love of the LORD never ends! By his mercies we have been kept from complete destruction. Great is his faithfulness; his mercies begin afresh each day. I say to myself, "The LORD is my inheritance; therefore, I will hope in him!" The LORD is wonderfully good to those who wait for him and seek him.*

Grief can renew your hope in God. In your grief, be encouraged that "the unfailing love of the LORD never ends!"

Psalm 30:11-12 *You have turned my mourning into joyful dancing. You have taken away my clothes of mourning and clothed me with joy, that I might sing praises to you and not be silent. O LORD my God, I will give you thanks forever!*

Grief can lead to a time of praise and thanksgiving to God.

2 Corinthians 1:4-6 *He comforts us in all our troubles so that we can comfort others. When others are troubled, we will be able to give them the same comfort God has given us. You can be sure that the more we suffer for Christ, the more God will shower us with his comfort through Christ. So when we are weighed down with troubles, it is for your benefit and salvation! For when God comforts us, it is so that we, in turn, can be an encouragement to you. Then you can patiently endure the same things we suffer.*
Grief can help you have the compassion and capability to comfort others. Grief is a teacher, which helps you learn to relate to others who are grieving.

How do I get over my grief?
Genesis 50:1 *Joseph threw himself on his father and wept over him.*

2 Samuel 18:33 *The king was overcome with emotion. He went up to his room over the gateway and burst into tears. And as he went, he cried, "O my son Absalom!"*
Recognize that grief is necessary and important. You need the freedom to grieve. It is an important part of closure because it allows you to honestly express the way you feel. Grief releases the emotional pressures of sorrow that come from loss.

Genesis 23:2-4 *There Abraham mourned and*

wept for her. Then, leaving her body, he went to the
Hittite elders and said, ". . . Please let me have a
piece of land for a burial plot."

Participate in the process of grief. Take time to
personally mourn, but also become involved in
the necessary steps to bring closure to your loss.
You are grieving because what you lost was
important to you. Expressing grief is a way of
honoring what was meaningful.

Ecclesiastes 3:1, 4 *There is a time for every-*
thing, a season for every activity under heaven. . . .
A time to cry and a time to laugh. A time to grieve
and a time to dance.

Grief has its season, and its season may last a
long while. But eventually God will lead you
to move on and comfort others who grieve.

Isaiah 66:13 *I will comfort you there as a child*
is comforted by its mother.

2 Corinthians 1:3 *He is the source of every*
mercy and the God who comforts us.

God knows you grieve, understands your sorrow,
and comforts you. He does not promise to
preserve us from grief, but to help us through it.

Revelation 21:4 *He will remove all of their*
sorrows, and there will be no more death or sorrow
or crying or pain.

Take hope that there will be no more grief in
heaven.

How can I help those who are grieving?

Psalm 69:20 *Their insults have broken my heart, and I am in despair. If only one person would show some pity; if only one would turn and comfort me.*

Proverbs 25:20 *Singing cheerful songs to a person whose heart is heavy is as bad as stealing someone's jacket in cold weather or rubbing salt in a wound.*

Romans 12:15 *When others are happy, be happy with them. If they are sad, share their sorrow.*
Give your attention, empathy, and comfort to the grieving. It is difficult to be with someone who is grieving, but you should realize that you don't need to come up with the right words to say to make it all go away. You can't. Your concern and presence will help the grieving person more than you can imagine.

PROMISE FROM GOD Psalm 34:18 *The LORD is close to the brokenhearted; he rescues those who are crushed in spirit.*

Hand of God

I don't see much evidence of "the hand of God" in the world today. Where is he? How does he work?

Psalm 66:5 *Come and see what our God has done, what awesome miracles he does for his people!*

God works on behalf of his people in miraculous ways. The news is filled with all the bad things that are happening. But if you take a moment and step back, you can begin to get a glimpse of God's quiet miracles working in many lives— even yours—every day. His hand is there, even when you don't see it.

Deuteronomy 4:34 *Has any other god taken one nation for himself by rescuing it from another by means of trials, miraculous signs, wonders, war, awesome power, and terrifying acts? Yet that is what the LORD your God did for you in Egypt, right before your very eyes.*

God works through trials, miraculous signs, wonders, war, awesome power, and even terrifying acts.

Daniel 6:27 *He rescues and saves his people; he performs miraculous signs and wonders in the heavens and on earth. He has rescued Daniel from the power of the lions.*

God works to rescue and save his people.

Jeremiah 31:35 *It is the LORD who provides the sun to light the day and the moon and stars to light the night. It is he who stirs the sea into roaring waves. His name is the LORD Almighty.*

Who but the Creator can control creation? All of creation is a testimony to the powerful hand of God. The fact that the sun comes up and warms you, that the rains water the land, that the seasons continue without fail reveal a God who still holds the world in his hand.

What does God's hand bring to me here in this world today?

James 1:17 *Whatever is good and perfect comes to us from God above, who created all heaven's lights.* Everything good and perfect that you experience comes from God's hand.

Job 2:10 *But Job replied, ". . . Should we accept only good things from the hand of God and never anything bad?"*
Sometimes God withdraws his hand and allows bad things to happen to good people. Why? Because his long-range eternal plans for your greater good may not fit your short-range view of comfort.

PROMISE FROM GOD Psalm 40:5 *O LORD my God, you have done many miracles for us. Your plans for us are too numerous to list. If I tried to recite all your wonderful deeds, I would never come to the end of them.*

Happiness

How can I be happy in the midst of these troubled times?

2 Corinthians 12:10 *Since I know it is all for*

Christ's good, I am quite content with my weaknesses and with insults, hardships, persecutions, and calamities. For when I am weak, then I am strong.

1 Peter 4:12-13 *Dear friends, don't be surprised at the fiery trials you are going through, as if something strange were happening to you. Instead, be very glad—because . . . you will have the wonderful joy of sharing his glory.*

Difficult circumstances help you to better understand what Christ went through for you.

Acts 5:41 *The apostles left the high council rejoicing that God had counted them worthy to suffer dishonor for the name of Jesus.*

Isaiah 52:7 *How beautiful on the mountains are the feet of those who bring good news of peace and salvation, the news that the God of Israel reigns!*

Happiness is living and sharing the wonderful news about the Lord. And during days like these, that's what people need more than anything else!

Daniel 12:3 *Those who are wise will shine as bright as the sky, and those who turn many to righteousness will shine like stars forever.*

You can be happy because you know that this world is not all there is. You know that something better is coming. So shine like a bright star in a dark sky. Let people see that, no matter what's happening in the world around you, you are happy in the knowledge of a future with your heavenly Father because of what Jesus has done for you. Your happiness may "turn many to righteousness"!

PROMISE FROM GOD Proverbs 11:23 *The godly can look forward to happiness, while the wicked can expect only wrath.*

Hatred

Is it ever appropriate to hate anyone or anything?

Leviticus 19:17 *Do not nurse hatred in your heart for any of your relatives.*

Psalm 97:10 *You who love the LORD, hate evil!*

1 John 3:15 *Anyone who hates another Christian is really a murderer at heart.*

Matthew 5:43-44 *You have heard that the law of Moses says, "Love your neighbor" and hate your enemy. But I say, love your enemies!*
Christians are to love all people and to hate all sin. When you truly love God, you will hate sin, because sin separates people from God and damages relationships with others. Hatred of people, however, is a sin. If you hate a person, you are most likely hating some kind of sin that that person committed against you. Hate the sin,

114

but ask God to give you love for the sinner by enabling you to pray for that person.

What causes unhealthy hatred?

Galatians 5:19, 22 *When you follow the desires of your sinful nature, your lives will produce these evil results. . . . But when the Holy Spirit controls our lives, he will produce this kind of fruit in us.*

Hatred comes from following our own sinful desires. Instead, allow the Holy Spirit to fill your life, leaving no room for hatred.

Esther 5:9 *What a happy man Haman was as he left the banquet! But when he saw Mordecai sitting at the gate, not standing up or trembling nervously before him, he was furious.*

Haman hated Mordecai because he refused to bow down before him. This petty jealousy, a hunger for recognition, drove Haman to insane hatred that would not be satisfied unless Mordecai was killed. Be careful! Petty jealousy can lead to hatred, which can lead to violent thoughts or actions.

How can I let go of hatred?

Proverbs 15:1 *A gentle answer turns away wrath, but harsh words stir up anger.*

Get rid of anger. Anger leads to bitterness, which leads to hatred.

Micah 6:8 *This is what he requires: to do what is right, to love mercy, and to walk humbly with your God.*
Mercy and humility are powerful weapons against hatred.

Ephesians 4:31-32 *Get rid of all bitterness. . . . Instead, be kind to each other, tenderhearted, forgiving one another.*
Forgiveness stops hatred.

Colossians 3:18-19 *You wives must submit to your husbands. . . . And you husbands must love your wives.*
Humble submission and love cast out hatred.

1 John 4:20 *If someone says, "I love God," but hates a Christian brother or sister, that person is a liar; for if we don't love people we can see, how can we love God, whom we have not seen?*
Genuinely nurturing your love for God will increase your love for others, and that love will conquer hatred.

PROMISE FROM GOD Psalm 45:7 *You love what is right and hate what is wrong. Therefore God, your God, has anointed you, pouring out the oil of joy on you more than on anyone else.*

Healing

How does God heal?

2 Kings 20:7 *"Make an ointment from figs and spread it over the boil." They did this, and Hezekiah recovered!*
Through physicians and medicine.

Luke 5:12-13 *"Lord," he said, "if you want to, you can make me well again." Jesus reached out and touched the man. "I want to," he said. "Be healed!"*
Through miracles.

Mark 2:4-5 *They couldn't get to Jesus through the crowd, so they dug through the clay roof above his head. . . . Seeing their faith, Jesus said to the paralyzed man, "My son, your sins are forgiven."*
Through the faith of friends.

Psalm 6:2 *Heal me, LORD, for my body is in agony.*

James 5:14 *Are any among you sick? They should call for the elders of the church and have them pray over them.*
Through prayer.

Isaiah 38:16 *Lord, your discipline is good, for it leads to life and health.*
Through discipline.

Genesis 27:41; 33:4 *Esau hated Jacob. . . . Then Esau ran to meet him and embraced him affectionately and kissed him. Both of them were in tears.*
Through time.

Isaiah 53:5 *He was wounded and crushed for our sins. He was beaten that we might have peace. He was whipped, and we were healed!*
Through Christ. His death brought you life; his wounds brought you healing. By accepting your punishment, he set you free.

Revelation 21:4 *He will remove all of their sorrows, and there will be no more death or sorrow or crying or pain. For the old world and its evils are gone forever.*
Through his promise of heaven. There you will receive complete and final healing.

Why doesn't God always heal people?

2 Corinthians 12:9 *My power works best in your weakness.*
We do not know why God heals some people and not others. We do know that God's power is magnified through our weaknesses and infirmities. If you have been praying to be healed—or praying for a loved one to be healed—and God has not done it, trust that he has something even greater that he wants to do through the illness.

How do I deal with it when I'm not healed?

2 Corinthians 12:10 *Since I know it is all for Christ's good, I am quite content with my weaknesses.*
You can look forward to having God's power work through you in a special way despite your weaknesses. When God works through your

weaknesses, it is obvious that what occurred happened because of him, thus showing the world his love and power.

PROMISE FROM GOD Malachi 4:2
But for you who fear my name, the Sun of Righteousness will rise with healing in his wings. And you will go free, leaping with joy like calves let out to pasture.

Heaven

Is there really a heaven?

John 14:2 *There are many rooms in my Father's home, and I am going to prepare a place for you. If this were not so, I would tell you plainly.*

2 Corinthians 5:1 *For we know that when this earthly tent we live in is taken down—when we die and leave these bodies—we will have a home in heaven.*

Not only is there a heaven, but Jesus is preparing it for your arrival.

What is heaven like?

Isaiah 65:17 *Look! I am creating new heavens and a new earth—so wonderful that no one will even think about the old ones anymore.*

Philippians 3:21 *He will take these weak mortal bodies of ours and change them into glorious bodies like his own.*

Revelation 21:3-4 *I heard a loud shout from the throne, saying, "Look, the home of God is now among his people! He will live with them, and they will be his people. God himself will be with them. He will remove all of their sorrows, and there will be no more death or sorrow or crying or pain. For the old world and its evils are gone forever."*

Revelation 22:5 *And there will be no night there—no need for lamps or sun—for the Lord God will shine on them. And they will reign forever and ever.*
Heaven is far beyond anything you can imagine. There will be no sadness, no pain, no evil, no death. Everything will be perfect and glorious. God will give you a new body, and you will be able to talk face-to-face with the Lord himself.

How can I be sure I will go to heaven?

John 3:16 *For God so loved the world that he gave his only Son, so that everyone who believes in him will not perish but have eternal life.*
If you have accepted Jesus Christ as Savior and recognize that only he can forgive your sins, you will gain entrance into heaven. You cannot earn your way to heaven, nor is it worth it even to try. Heaven is God's gift to those who trust in Jesus.

PROMISE FROM GOD 1 Corinthians 2:9 *No eye has seen, no ear has heard, and no mind has imagined what God has prepared for those who love him.*

Help

I need help. What kind of help can I expect to get from God?

2 Chronicles 15:4 *But whenever you were in distress and turned to the LORD . . . and sought him out, you found him.*
God is present to help you whenever you call to him. Prayer is the lifeline that connects you to the Lord God your helper.

Philippians 4:19 *This same God who takes care of me will supply all your needs from his glorious riches, which have been given to us in Christ Jesus.*
God has a full supply house and a ready supply system. It's free for the asking, but you must ask.

Psalm 28:7 *The LORD is my strength, my shield from every danger. I trust in him with all my heart. He helps me, and my heart is filled with joy.*
God protects you from the enemy and gives you spiritual victory.

Isaiah 30:21 *You will hear a voice say, "This is the way; turn around and walk here."*
God guides you by his Holy Spirit.

Romans 8:26 *The Holy Spirit helps us in our distress. For we don't even know what we should pray for, nor how we should pray. But the Holy Spirit prays for us with groanings that cannot be expressed in words.*

God helps you to pray, even when you don't know how or don't know what to say.

Lots of people around me need help. How can I help them?

Genesis 14:14, 16 *When Abram learned that Lot had been captured, he called together the men born into his household. . . . Abram and his allies recovered everything.*
If your brother or sister is in danger, you should do whatever you can to help and, if necessary, rescue him or her.

Acts 16:9 *That night Paul had a vision. He saw a man from Macedonia in northern Greece, pleading with him, "Come over here and help us."*
You can tell others the Good News of Christ, giving them an opportunity to be saved from judgment.

Acts 20:28 *Be sure that you feed and shepherd God's flock—his church, purchased with his blood— over whom the Holy Spirit has appointed you as elders.*
You can help other believers to grow to maturity in Christ.

Romans 12:13 *When God's children are in need, be the one to help them out. And get into the habit of inviting guests home for dinner or, if they need lodging, for the night.*
You can help by being hospitable in very practical ways.

Galatians 6:1 *If another Christian is overcome by some sin, you who are godly should gently and humbly help that person back onto the right path.* When another believer has fallen into sin, you should help restore him.

PROMISE FROM GOD Matthew 28:20 *Be sure of this: I am with you always, even to the end of the age.*

Helplessness

(*see also* STRENGTH)

What can I do when I feel helpless?

Hebrews 13:6 *The Lord is my helper, so I will not be afraid. What can mere mortals do to me?* Meditate on God's limitless power and steadfast love for you, reminding yourself that the Lord is far greater than any problem confronting you.

Psalm 18:6 *But in my distress I cried out to the LORD; yes, I prayed to my God for help. He heard me from his sanctuary; my cry reached his ears.* Pray consistently and confidently for God's help.

1 Peter 5:12 *I have written this short letter to you with the help of Silas, whom I consider a faithful brother.* Stay connected to other Christians and let them

know how they can support you. Don't be too proud to ask people for help.

Deuteronomy 24:18 *Always remember that you were slaves in Egypt and that the LORD your God redeemed you.*

Take time to reflect on past situations when you felt helpless but the Lord helped you. God's track record in your life can increase your confidence today.

How does God help me when I feel helpless?

Isaiah 41:10, 13-14 *Don't be afraid, for I am with you. Do not be dismayed, for I am your God. I will strengthen you. I will help you. I will uphold you with my victorious right hand. . . . I am holding you by your right hand—I, the LORD your God. And I say to you, "Do not be afraid. I am here to help you. Despised though you are, O Israel, don't be afraid, for I will help you. I am the LORD, your Redeemer. I am the Holy One of Israel."*

Psalm 115:9-11 *O Israel, trust the LORD! He is your helper; he is your shield. O priests of Aaron, trust the LORD! He is your helper; he is your shield. All you who fear the LORD, trust the LORD! He is your helper; he is your shield.*

God is your refuge, strength, and shield. His help is active, not passive—he rescues, he protects, and he strengthens.

Psalm 142:3 *I am overwhelmed, and you alone know the way I should turn. Wherever I go, my enemies have set traps for me.*
God gives direction. He who knows the way will lead you.

1 Thessalonians 2:2 *You know how badly we had been treated at Philippi just before we came to you and how much we suffered there. Yet our God gave us the courage to declare his Good News to you boldly, even though we were surrounded by many who opposed us.*
God gives courage in the face of opposition.

1 Samuel 12:8 *When the Israelites were in Egypt and cried out to the LORD, he sent Moses and Aaron to rescue them from Egypt and to bring them into this land.*
God sends others to help. He who sees your helplessness sends helpers.

Deuteronomy 7:21-24 *No, do not be afraid of those nations, for the LORD your God is among you, and he is a great and awesome God. The LORD your God will drive those nations out ahead of you little by little. You will not clear them away all at once, for if you did, the wild animals would multiply too quickly for you. But the LORD your God will hand them over to you. He will throw them into complete confusion until they are destroyed. He will put their kings in your power, and you will erase their names* *from the face of the earth. No one will be able to stand against you, and you will destroy them all.* Sometimes God's help is a gradual process; otherwise we might not appreciate it or couldn't handle it. God's timing brings the most help at the best time.

How can I maintain hope when I feel helpless in the face of discouraging circumstances?

Daniel 3:21, 23, 27-28 *So they tied them up and threw them into the furnace, fully clothed.... So Shadrach, Meshach, and Abednego, securely tied, fell down into the roaring flames.... Not a hair on their heads was singed, and their clothing was not scorched. They didn't even smell of smoke! Then Nebuchadnezzar said, "Praise to the God of Shadrach, Meshach, and Abednego! He sent his angel to rescue his servants who trusted in him. They defied the king's command and were willing to die rather than serve or worship any god except their own God.* Don't panic! Start praying. You'll discover God's presence.

Matthew 6:27-30, 32-34 *Can all your worries add a single moment to your life? Of course not.... Look at the lilies and how they grow. They don't work or make their clothing, yet Solomon in all his glory was not dressed as beautifully as they are. And if God cares so wonderfully for flowers that are*

here today and gone tomorrow, won't he more surely care for you? . . . Your heavenly Father already knows all your needs, and he will give you all you need from day to day if you live for him and make the Kingdom of God your primary concern. So don't worry about tomorrow, for tomorrow will bring its own worries. Today's trouble is enough for today.
Focus on God. Keep praying. You'll discover God's peace.

Romans 12:12 *Be glad for all God is planning for you. Be patient in trouble, and always be prayerful.*
Remember God is sovereign and loving. Be patient and prayerful. You'll discover the joy of knowing he cares for you.

Romans 15:4 *Such things were written in the Scriptures long ago to teach us. They give us hope and encouragement as we wait patiently for God's promises.*
Read God's Word. Learn how to apply it to your life. You'll discover the power of God's promises.

Psalm 27:14 *Wait patiently for the LORD. Be brave and courageous. Yes, wait patiently for the LORD.*

Isaiah 40:31 *But those who wait on the LORD will find new strength. They will fly high on wings like eagles. They will run and not grow weary. They will walk and not faint.*
Wait quietly and patiently for God to work. You'll discover he always comes through.

PROMISE FROM GOD Psalm 118:7
Yes, the LORD is for me; he will help me.

Hope

Where does hope come from?

Psalm 39:7 *And so, Lord, where do I put my hope? My only hope is in you.*
The Lord himself is the source of hope because his character is unchanging, his love is steadfast, his promises will all come true, and his omnipotence determines your future.

Why should I place my hope in God?

Hebrews 6:18-19 *So God has given us both his promise and his oath. These two things are unchangeable because it is impossible for God to lie. Therefore, we who have fled to him for refuge can take new courage, for we can hold on to his promise with confidence. This confidence is like a strong and trustworthy anchor for our souls. It leads us through the curtain of heaven into God's inner sanctuary.*
God cannot lie because he *is* truth. God, therefore, cannot break his promises. His Word stands forever. God alone provides lasting hope because he alone conquered death by raising Christ from the dead.

How can I keep hoping when God never seems to act?

Romans 8:24-25 *If you already have something, you don't need to hope for it. But if we look forward to something we don't have yet, we must wait patiently and confidently.*

Hope, by definition, is expecting something that has not yet occurred. Once hope is fulfilled, it isn't hope anymore. Thus, the practical outworking of hope is patience.

Where can I go to strengthen my hope?

Psalm 119:43, 74, 81, 114, 147 *Do not snatch your word of truth from me, for my only hope is in your laws. . . . May all who fear you find in me a cause for joy, for I have put my hope in your word. . . . I faint with longing for your salvation; but I have put my hope in your word. . . . You are my refuge and my shield; your word is my only source of hope. . . . I rise early, before the sun is up; I cry out for help and put my hope in your words.*

Each day you can read God's Word and have your hope renewed and reinforced. His Word never fails.

What can I do when things seem hopeless?

1 Samuel 1:10 *Hannah was in deep anguish, crying bitterly as she prayed to the LORD.*

You can pray. In the midst of Hannah's hopelessness, she prayed to God, knowing that if any hope were to be found, it would be found in him.

ACTS 16:24-25 *He took no chances but put them into the inner dungeon and clamped their feet in the stocks. Around midnight, Paul and Silas were praying and singing hymns to God.*
You can worship. Paul and Silas were on death row for preaching about Jesus, yet in this hopeless situation they sang praises to God. This reinforced an eternal perspective.

PROVERBS 10:28 *The hopes of the godly result in happiness, but the expectations of the wicked are all in vain.*
You can focus on eternity. No matter how hopeless things seem here on earth, in Christ you have ultimate, eternal hope. People who don't know Christ have nothing but a hopeless view of the future. You have been promised great hope, so cling to those promises.

PSALM 27:14 *Wait patiently for the LORD. Be brave and courageous.*
You can remember that God's timing is perfect.

HAGGAI 1:9 *You hoped for rich harvests, but they were poor. And when you brought your harvest home, I blew it away. Why? Because my house lies in ruins, says the LORD Almighty, while you are all busy building your own fine houses.*
You can persist in putting God first.

Psalm 18:4-6 *The ropes of death surrounded me; the floods of destruction swept over me. The grave wrapped its ropes around me; death itself stared me in the face. But in my distress I cried out to the LORD; yes, I prayed to my God for help. He heard me from his sanctuary; my cry reached his ears.*

You can remember that sin and evil may sometimes thwart your plans here on earth, but it cannot affect God's plans in heaven.

PROMISE FROM GOD Jeremiah 29:11 *"I know the plans I have for you," says the LORD. "They are plans for good and not for disaster, to give you a future and a hope."*

Hostility

How can I have peace instead of hostility?

John 16:33 *I have told you all this so that you may have peace in me. Here on earth you will have many trials and sorrows. But take heart, because I have overcome the world.*

The secret of finding peace is to first seek it from the Prince of Peace. Peace is a gift from God, experienced initially as we accept his Son and daily as we allow his Spirit to guide us as we follow God's Word and his ways. You can find the secret to peace in a personal relationship with Jesus Christ.

131

2 Peter 3:14 *And so, dear friends, while you are waiting for these things to happen, make every effort to live a pure and blameless life. And be at peace with God.*

Romans 12:18 *Do your part to live in peace with everyone, as much as possible.*

Matthew 5:9 *God blesses those who work for peace, for they will be called the children of God.* Make peace a priority in your relationships— first with God, and then with others.

PROMISE FROM GOD 2 Samuel 22:3, 49 *My God is my rock, in whom I find protection. He is my shield, the strength of my salvation, and my stronghold, my high tower, my savior, the one who saves me from violence. . . . and rescues me from my enemies. You hold me safe beyond the reach of my enemies; you save me from violent opponents.*

Hurts/Hurting

(*see also* BROKENHEARTED or GRIEF or SORROW or SUFFERING)

When I've been hurt, how can I find healing?

Ecclesiastes 3:4 *A time to cry and a time to laugh. A time to grieve and a time to dance.*

2 Corinthians 2:4 *How painful it was to write that letter! Heartbroken, I cried over it. I didn't want to hurt you, but I wanted you to know how very much I love you.*
You need to express your pain—privately to God, to a friend, or even publicly. Unexpressed pain can fester within you, driving you toward many unwanted emotions like depression or bitterness.

Psalm 22:24 *He has not ignored the suffering of the needy. He has not turned and walked away. He has listened to their cries for help.*

Psalm 119:76 *Now let your unfailing love comfort me, just as you promised me, your servant.*
God compassionately cares for you. Meditate on the attributes of his character and recognize that the one who made you is the best one to heal you.

Psalm 19:8 *The commandments of the LORD are right, bringing joy to the heart. The commands of the LORD are clear, giving insight to life.*
Look to God's Word, the Bible, as a source of comfort and healing. These are the words of God himself, and there is much there about turning your hurts into healing.

Psalm 126:5-6 *Those who plant in tears will harvest with shouts of joy. They weep as they go to plant their seed, but they sing as they return with the harvest.*

Romans 8:23 *And even we Christians, although we have the Holy Spirit within us as a foretaste of future glory, also groan to be released from pain and suffering. We, too, wait anxiously for that day when God will give us our full rights as his children, including the new bodies he has promised us.*

God does not promise believers a life without pain or suffering. If Christians didn't hurt, people would turn to God as a magic potion to take away their pain. The difference is that Christians have a relationship with God that helps us through our hurts, comforts us in our hurts, and sometimes miraculously heals our hurts. But most important, we have a God who will take away all of our hurts when we arrive at heaven's doorstep. Whatever pain you are experiencing is temporal; it will end.

Genesis 33:4 *Esau ran to meet him and embraced him affectionately and kissed him. Both of them were in tears.*

Forgiveness is like a miracle medicine to heal our brokenness. Accept it gladly.

How can God use my pain and my hurtful situations to glorify himself?

2 Corinthians 12:9-10 *Each time he said, "My gracious favor is all you need. My power works best in your weakness." So now I am glad to boast about my weaknesses, so that the power of Christ may work through me. Since I know it is all for Christ's*

134

good, I am quite content with my weaknesses and with insults, hardships, persecutions, and calamities. For when I am weak, then I am strong.
God can use your weakness and pain to reveal his strength and power. It is often through pain that you most vividly experience God's work in your life.

2 Corinthians 4:18 *We don't look at the troubles we can see right now; rather, we look forward to what we have not yet seen. For the troubles we see will soon be over, but the joys to come will last forever.*
God can use your pain to help you gain an eternal perspective.

1 Peter 4:1 *Since Christ suffered physical pain, you must arm yourselves with the same attitude he had, and be ready to suffer, too. For if you are willing to suffer for Christ, you have decided to stop sinning.*
God can use your pain as an opportunity for you to demonstrate your loyalty to him.

1 Peter 1:7 *These trials are only to test your faith, to show that it is strong and pure. It is being tested as fire tests and purifies gold—and your faith is far more precious to God than mere gold. So if your faith remains strong after being tried by fiery trials, it will bring you much praise and glory and honor on the day when Jesus Christ is revealed to the whole world.*

Romans 5:3-4 *We can rejoice, too, when we run into problems and trials, for we know that they are*

good for us—they help us learn to endure. And endurance develops strength of character in us, and character strengthens our confident expectation of salvation.
Hurtful situations can strengthen your faith, test your endurance, and mold your character.

James 4:9 *Let there be tears for the wrong things you have done. Let there be sorrow and deep grief. Let there be sadness instead of laughter, and gloom instead of joy.*

Psalm 51:17 *The sacrifice you want is a broken spirit. A broken and repentant heart, O God, you will not despise.*
God can use painful situations to bring about personal remorse and a change of your ways to his.

Hebrews 12:11 *No discipline is enjoyable while it is happening—it is painful! But afterward there will be a quiet harvest of right living for those who are trained in this way.*
God can use painful discipline to help you make the right choices in the future.

Psalm 41:3 *The LORD nurses them when they are sick and eases their pain and discomfort.*
Pain is an opportunity for God to minister to his people. Don't miss the opportunity when it comes.

How should I respond to those who hurt me?

Matthew 6:14-15 *If you forgive those who sin against you, your heavenly Father will forgive you.*

136

But if you refuse to forgive others, your Father will not forgive your sins.

M a r k   1 1 : 2 5 *When you are praying, first forgive anyone you are holding a grudge against, so that your Father in heaven will forgive your sins, too.* Forgiveness is not an option; it is a command. It is necessary for the health of your own relationship with God. Jesus gave us the perfect example of forgiveness to follow. Forgiving doesn't mean you say that the hurt doesn't exist or that it doesn't matter, nor does it make everything "all right." Forgiveness allows you to let go of the one who hurt you and let God deal with that person. Forgiveness sets you free. Forgiveness allows you to put the past in the past and move on with your life. It won't be easy, but forgiving others for the hurt they have caused you is the most healthy thing you can do for yourself.

G e n e s i s   5 0 : 1 5 ,   1 9 - 2 1 *But now that their father was dead, Joseph's brothers became afraid. "Now Joseph will pay us back for all the evil we did to him," they said. . . . But Joseph told them, "Don't be afraid of me. Am I God, to judge and punish you? As far as I am concerned, God turned into good what you meant for evil. He brought me to the high position I have today so I could save the lives of many people. No, don't be afraid. Indeed, I myself will take care of you and your families." And he spoke very kindly to them, reassuring them.*

You must wait for the Lord to do things his way.
God wants you to respond in love with a blessing
rather than retaliation.

How can I help people who are hurting?

Psalm 69:20 *Their insults have broken my heart,
and I am in despair. If only one person would show
some pity; if only one would turn and comfort me.*

1 Peter 3:8 *Finally, all of you should be of one
mind, full of sympathy toward each other, loving one
another with tender hearts and humble minds.*
You can give your attention, empathy, and
comfort to the brokenhearted. Insults and cruel
words are abrasive, wounding the heart. Attention, empathy, and comfort are therapeutic,
healing the heart.

Proverbs 15:13 *A glad heart makes a happy
face; a broken heart crushes the spirit.*

Job 30:16 *And now my heart is broken. Depression haunts my days.*

Proverbs 17:22 *A cheerful heart is good
medicine, but a broken spirit saps a person's strength.*
You can be aware of the effects of being brokenhearted on a person's spirit, mind, and body.
Awareness leads to sympathy; sympathy leads to
empathy; empathy leads to helping the wounded,
and that leads to a time of healing.

Romans 12:15 *When others are happy, be happy
with them. If they are sad, share their sorrow.*

1 Corinthians 12:26 *If one part suffers, all the parts suffer with it, and if one part is honored, all the parts are glad.*

Hebrews 13:3 *Don't forget about those in prison. Suffer with them as though you were there yourself. Share the sorrow of those being mistreated, as though you feel their pain in your own bodies.*
You can share in others' sorrows as surely as you can share in their joy.

2 Corinthians 1:4 *He comforts us in all our troubles so that we can comfort others. When others are troubled, we will be able to give them the same comfort God has given us.*
You can share your experiences of God's comfort. In the pattern of God's healing, others may find healing in you.

1 Peter 5:12 *I have written this short letter to you with the help of Silas, whom I consider a faithful brother. My purpose in writing is to encourage you and assure you that the grace of God is with you no matter what happens.*
You can encourage the brokenhearted. Words of comfort can lift up the hurting person.

Proverbs 12:18 *Some people make cutting remarks, but the words of the wise bring healing.*

Job 2:13 *Then they sat on the ground with him for seven days and nights. And no one said a word, for they saw that his suffering was too great for words.*

You can be careful about the words you speak to the brokenhearted. Explanations and clichés are rarely comforting. Love, sympathy, and the power of your presence are urgently needed. Sometimes the best comfort you can give is to just be there. Words are less important than the person who says them and the way they are spoken.

1 Thessalonians 3:7 *We have been greatly comforted, dear brothers and sisters, in all of our own crushing troubles and suffering, because you have remained strong in your faith.*

Romans 1:12 *I'm eager to encourage you in your faith, but I also want to be encouraged by yours. In this way, each of us will be a blessing to the other.* You can remain strong in your own faith. Those weakened by hurt are encouraged to see those strengthened by overcoming their hurt.

Job 42:11 *Then all his brothers, sisters, and former friends came and feasted with him in his home. And they consoled him and comforted him because of all the trials the Lord had brought against him. And each of them brought him a gift of money and a gold ring.*

Psalm 68:6 *God places the lonely in families; he sets the prisoners free and gives them joy. But for rebels, there is only famine and distress.*

Mark 16:10 *She went and found the disciples, who were grieving and weeping.*

As family and friends, you can support one another. Family life must be a safe haven from a wounding world. The family haven should be both a healing clinic and a training camp where family members learn to cope with and to conquer wounding influences.

PROMISE FROM GOD Revelation 21:4 *He will remove all of their sorrows, and there will be no more death or sorrow or crying or pain. For the old world and its evils are gone forever.*

Impossible

Can God really do the impossible?

Zechariah 8:6 *This is what the LORD Almighty says: All this may seem impossible to you now, a small and discouraged remnant of God's people. But do you think this is impossible for me, the LORD Almighty?*

Matthew 19:26 *Jesus looked at them intently and said, "Humanly speaking, it is impossible. But with God everything is possible."*

Luke 1:37 *For nothing is impossible with God.* There should be no doubt that God specializes in doing things that are impossible from a human perspective. The God who spoke all creation into being can do miracles for you.

How do I deal with impossible situations?

Judges 4:3 *Sisera, who had nine hundred iron chariots, ruthlessly oppressed the Israelites for twenty years. Then the Israelites cried out to the Lord for help.*

2 Kings 19:1 *When King Hezekiah heard their report, he tore his clothes and put on sackcloth and went into the Temple of the LORD to pray.*
Go immediately to God in prayer. What choice do you have but to go to the only one who can do the impossible?

Proverbs 3:5 *Trust in the LORD with all your heart; do not depend on your own understanding.*

Psalm 60:12 *With God's help we will do mighty things, for he will trample down our foes.*

Mark 9:23 *"What do you mean, 'If I can'?" Jesus asked. "Anything is possible if a person believes."*
Place your faith and hope in God alone. Trust that God can do the impossible and have hope that he will. But even if he doesn't, believe that he is the only one who can.

Revelation 3:8 *I know all the things you do, and I have opened a door for you that no one can shut. You have little strength, yet you obeyed my word and did not deny me.*

1 Chronicles 28:20 *Then David continued, "Be strong and courageous, and do the work. Don't be afraid or discouraged by the size of the task, for the*

LORD God, my God, is with you. He will not fail you or forsake you. He will see to it that all the work related to the Temple of the LORD is finished correctly."
Start by doing what you can—obey his Word, the Bible! When you live by God's principles, you remain in the protection of his helping arms.

Daniel 2:11, 27-28 *"This is an impossible thing the king requires. No one except the gods can tell you your dream, and they do not live among people." . . . Daniel replied, "There are no wise men, enchanters, magicians, or fortune-tellers who can tell the king such things. But there is a God in heaven who reveals secrets, and he has shown King Nebuchadnezzar what will happen in the future. Now I will tell you your dream and the visions you saw as you lay on your bed."*
Only God can do the impossible, but he often allows his people to be involved in his work. Be ready to be used to accomplish whatever God has in mind!

How does God use impossible situations to accomplish his will?

Numbers 11:23 *Then the LORD said to Moses, "Is there any limit to my power? Now you will see whether or not my word comes true!"*
God uses the impossible to remind you that he is God and you are not. Then you can trust him more fully.

Exodus 10:1 *Then the LORD said to Moses, "Return to Pharaoh and again make your demands. I have made him and his officials stubborn so I can continue to display my power by performing miraculous signs among them."*
God uses the impossible to display his character and his unlimited power.

Psalm 66:5 *Come and see what our God has done, what awesome miracles he does for his people!*
God uses the impossible to draw people to him.

Psalm 89:5 *All heaven will praise your miracles, LORD; myriads of angels will praise you for your faithfulness.*
God uses the impossible to prepare people to praise him. Your limitations prepare you to praise the God of no limitations.

Psalm 65:5 *You faithfully answer our prayers with awesome deeds, O God our savior. You are the hope of everyone on earth, even those who sail on distant seas.*

Psalm 78:7 *Each generation can set its hope anew on God, remembering his glorious miracles and obeying his commands.*
While impossibilities limit people and exhaust all human resources, they are the stage on which God is at his best—loving us, bringing salvation, changing lives, and meeting needs—for everyone on earth, for all generations.

PROMISE FROM GOD Ephesians 3 : 2 0 *Now glory be to God! By his mighty power at work within us, he is able to accomplish infinitely more than we would ever dare to ask or hope.*

Injustice

Why does a loving, sovereign God allow injustice? Why doesn't he stop it?

Psalm 9 : 1 6 *The LORD is known for his justice. The wicked have trapped themselves in their own snares.*

Lamentations 3 : 3 6 *They perverted justice in the courts. Do they think the Lord didn't see it?*

Job 3 6 : 6 , 1 7 *He does not let the wicked live but gives justice to the afflicted. . . . But you are too obsessed with judgment on the godless. Don't worry, justice will be upheld.*

Injustice happens because God created human beings with the ability to choose between doing good or evil, right or wrong. If God hadn't done it that way, we would only be puppets of a divine dictator, not people who love him. God knew that people needed the freedom to choose, but that also means that many will choose wrongly, causing injustice to the innocent. God, however, does not condone injustice; he sees every injustice and judges it to be sin.

What will God do about injustice?

Psalm 10:18 *You will bring justice to the orphans and the oppressed, so people can no longer terrify them.*

Psalm 12:5 *The LORD replies, "I have seen violence done to the helpless, and I have heard the groans of the poor. Now I will rise up to rescue them, as they have longed for me to do."*

Psalm 37:28 *For the LORD loves justice, and he will never abandon the godly. He will keep them safe forever, but the children of the wicked will perish.*

Colossians 3:25 *But if you do what is wrong, you will be paid back for the wrong you have done. For God has no favorites who can get away with evil.*

God will punish all who persist in doing what is unjust and sinful. Some begin to experience their punishment on earth, and others will receive their full punishment in eternity. Our just and holy God cannot and will not allow injustice to go unpunished.

What should I do about injustice in the world?

Hebrews 13:3 *Don't forget about those in prison. Suffer with them as though you were there yourself. Share the sorrow of those being mistreated, as though you feel their pain in your own bodies.*

Don't ignore those being treated unjustly. Reach out to them in their distress and seek justice on their behalf.

Psalm 82:3 *Give fair judgment to the poor and the orphan; uphold the rights of the oppressed and the destitute.*

Proverbs 31:8-9 *Speak up for those who cannot speak for themselves; ensure justice for those who are perishing. Yes, speak up for the poor and helpless, and see that they get justice.*
Speak out on behalf of those being treated unjustly. Silence toward injustice is unjust. It is amazing how speaking up often makes a difference.

Isaiah 1:17 *Learn to do good. Seek justice. Help the oppressed. Defend the orphan. Fight for the rights of widows.*

Job 29:16 *I was a father to the poor and made sure that even strangers received a fair trial.*

Proverbs 24:11-12 *Rescue those who are unjustly sentenced to death; don't stand back and let them die. Don't try to avoid responsibility by saying you didn't know about it. For God knows all hearts, and he sees you. He keeps watch over your soul, and he knows you knew! And he will judge all people according to what they have done.*
Step out in action.

Psalm 58:10 *The godly will rejoice when they see injustice avenged. They will wash their feet in the blood of the wicked.*

1 Corinthians 13:6 *[Love] is never glad about injustice but rejoices whenever the truth wins out.* Celebrate when justice prevails. Injustice requires mourning; justice requires celebration.

PROMISE FROM GOD Psalm 9:8 *He will judge the world with justice and rule the nations with fairness.*

Intercession

(*see also* PRAYER)

Does it really make a difference when others are praying for me or I am praying for others?

2 Corinthians 1:11 *He will rescue us because you are helping by praying for us.*

Paul was convinced that the Corinthians' prayers were vitally connected to his deliverance by God. Intercession is the practice of praying for the needs of others. It is easy to become discouraged if you think there is nothing anyone can do for you—or nothing that you can do to help someone you care about. But in fact, the most important thing you can do for others, and others can do for you, is to pray. In ways beyond our under-standing, intercessory prayer is a channel for the love and power of God, and creates a deep bond of fellowship between fellow believers.

Acts 12:5 *While Peter was in prison, the church prayed very earnestly for him.*
Even as the believers were holding an all-night prayer meeting, God sent an angel to rescue Peter from prison.

Genesis 18:32 *Finally, Abraham said, "Lord, please do not get angry; I will speak but once more! Suppose only ten are found there?" And the LORD said, "Then, for the sake of the ten, I will not destroy it."*
Abraham interceded earnestly for an entire city.

What can I ask for when I'm interceding for someone?

3 John 2 *Dear friend, I am praying that all is well with you and that your body is as healthy as I know your soul is.*
You can pray for the person's everyday, practical needs.

1 Samuel 1:17 *May the God of Israel grant the request you have asked of him.*
You can pray that God will satisfy the deepest longings of the person's heart.

Romans 15:31 *Pray that I will be rescued from those in Judea who refuse to obey God.*

You can pray for the person to be delivered from a crisis.

Acts 8:24 *"Pray to the Lord for me," Simon exclaimed, "that these terrible things won't happen to me!"*
You can pray for the person's salvation.

Ephesians 3:14-16 *When I think of the wisdom and scope of God's plan, I fall to my knees and pray to the Father, the Creator of everything in heaven and on earth. I pray that from his glorious, unlimited resources he will give you mighty inner strength through his Holy Spirit.*
You can pray for the person's spiritual growth and strength.

Colossians 4:3-4 *Don't forget to pray for us, too, that God will give us many opportunities to preach about his secret plan—that Christ is also for you Gentiles. That is why I am here in chains. Pray that I will proclaim this message as clearly as I should.*
You can pray not only that God might change the person's circumstances but also that God will enable that person to serve him effectively even if the circumstances do not change.

PROMISE FROM GOD James 5:16 *The earnest prayer of a righteous person has great power and wonderful results.*

Joy

Does God promise me happiness?

Philippians 4:4,12 *Always be full of joy in the Lord. I say it again—rejoice! . . . I have learned the secret of living in every situation.*

James 1:2 *Whenever trouble comes your way, let it be an opportunity for joy.*

God does not promise temporary happiness; in fact, the Bible assumes problems will come your way. But God does promise lasting joy for all those who believe in him. This kind of joy stays with you despite your problems.

What is the source of joy?

Psalm 40:16 *But may all who search for you be filled with joy and gladness. May those who love your salvation repeatedly shout, "The LORD is great!"*

Psalm 68:3 *Let the godly rejoice. Let them be glad in God's presence. Let them be filled with joy.*

The Lord himself is the wellspring of true joy. The more you love him, know him, walk with him, and become like him, the greater your joy.

How can I become more joyful?

Hebrews 12:2 *We do this by keeping our eyes on Jesus. . . . He was willing to die a shameful death on the cross because of the joy he knew would be his afterward.* Keep your eyes on Jesus.

Psalm 112:1 *Happy are those who fear the LORD. Yes, happy are those who delight in doing what he commands.*
Fear God and trust in him; delight in doing his commands.

Psalm 16:8-9 *I know the LORD is always with me. . . . No wonder my heart is filled with joy.*
Joy comes from an awareness of God's presence, which brings true contentment.

Galatians 5:22 *But when the Holy Spirit controls our lives, he will produce this kind of fruit in us: love, joy . . .*
The presence of the Holy Spirit in your life produces joy.

Psalm 119:2 *Happy are those who obey his decrees and search for him with all their hearts.*

Philippians 1:25 *I will continue with you so that you will grow and experience the joy of your faith.*
God has promised that when you truly seek him, you will surely find him, and when you find him, your joy will be complete.

Matthew 25:21 *You have been faithful in handling this small amount. . . . Let's celebrate together!*
Serving God well brings a deep sense of satisfaction and is an occasion for joy.

How can I be joyful in the midst of difficult circumstances?

2 Corinthians 12:10 *Since I know it is all for Christ's good, I am quite content with my weaknesses and with insults, hardships, persecutions, and calamities. For when I am weak, then I am strong.*

1 Peter 4:12-13 *Dear friends, don't be surprised at the fiery trials you are going through, as if something strange were happening to you. Instead, be very glad—because . . . you will have the wonderful joy of sharing his glory.*

Difficult circumstances help you better understand what Christ went through for you. They make you partners with him.

Romans 5:2 *We confidently and joyfully look forward to sharing God's glory.*

Hebrews 10:34 *When all you owned was taken from you, you accepted it with joy. You knew you had better things waiting for you in eternity.*

Hope in God's promises of eternal life can make you joyful because you know that what you are presently going through will one day end.

Acts 5:41 *The apostles left the high council rejoicing that God had counted them worthy to suffer dishonor for the name of Jesus.*

Doing something significant for God, even though you may suffer for it, brings great joy because you know that God is working through you to accomplish something important for his kingdom. You experience joy when you know that God is pleased with you and that your work for him will bring a reward in heaven.

PROMISE FROM GOD Nehemiah 8:10 *The joy of the LORD is your strength!*

Justice

Is God always fair and just?

2 Thessalonians 1:5-6 *But God will use this persecution to show his justice. . . . and in his justice he will punish those who persecute you.*
When you are burdened with troubles, it is tempting to think that God is not fair or just. How can God allow a Christian to suffer when so many unbelievers are prospering? But rest assured that God's justice will eventually prevail.

The world seems so unjust. Will God's justice really prevail?

Psalm 96:12-13 *Let the trees of the forest rustle with praise before the LORD! For the LORD is coming! He is coming to judge the earth. He will judge the world with righteousness, and all the nations with his truth.*
Complete justice will occur only when Jesus returns as judge. Make no mistake: This is his solemn promise, and it is certain.

Matthew 6:10 *May your Kingdom come soon. May your will be done here on earth, just as it is in heaven.*
Through the work of his church, God's kingdom is advancing in the world now. Though complete justice will come only in the future, we can—and must—work for justice in our own spheres of influence. With God's help, justice will increase.

PROMISE FROM GOD Romans 12:19 *Never avenge yourselves. Leave that to God. For it is written, "I will take vengeance; I will repay those who deserve it," says the Lord.*

Limitations

Does God have any limitations?
Psalm 139:1-6 *O LORD, you have examined my heart and know everything about me. You know when I sit down or stand up. You know my every thought when far away. You chart the path ahead of me and tell me where to stop and rest. Every moment you know where I am. You know what I am going to say even before I say it, LORD. You both precede and follow me. You place your hand of blessing on my head. Such knowledge is too wonderful for me, too great for me to know!*

Isaiah 55:8 *"My thoughts are completely different from yours," says the LORD. "And my ways are far beyond anything you could imagine."*
God's knowledge has no limit. He is omniscient. He knows even our secret thoughts.

Numbers 11:23 *The LORD said to Moses, "Is there any limit to my power? Now you will see whether or not my word comes true!"*

Job 37:5 *God's voice is glorious in the thunder. We cannot comprehend the greatness of his power.*

Matthew 19:26 *Jesus looked at them intently and said, "Humanly speaking, it is impossible. But with God everything is possible."*
There is no limitation to God's power and strength. He is omnipotent. No problem is too great for him to solve.

Psalm 139:7-10 *I can never escape from your spirit! I can never get away from your presence! If I go up to heaven, you are there; if I go down to the place of the dead, you are there. If I ride the wings of the morning, if I dwell by the farthest oceans, even there your hand will guide me, and your strength will support me.*
God's presence has no limit. He is omnipresent. No place is too far away for God.

John 5:19-21 *Jesus replied, ". . . Whatever the Father does, the Son also does. For the Father loves the Son and tells him everything he is doing, and the*

*Son will do far greater things than healing this man.
You will be astonished at what he does. He will even
raise from the dead anyone he wants to, just as the
Father does."*

God's authority has no limit. No deed is too great
for him to do.

Isaiah 40:28 *No one can measure the depths
of his understanding.*

God's knowledge has no limit. It is futile for
us—mere humans—to attempt to understand
all about God. We cannot. His knowledge and
understanding are beyond us.

Job 9:10 *His great works are too marvelous to
understand. He performs miracles without number.*

Psalm 92:5 *O LORD, what great miracles you do!
And how deep are your thoughts.*

God's work has no limit. His plans cannot be
stopped. There is no miracle too awesome for
him to perform.

Psalm 119:96 *Even perfection has its limits,
but your commands have no limit.*

Isaiah 55:11 *It is the same with my word.
I send it out, and it always produces fruit. It will
accomplish all I want it to, and it will prosper everywhere I send it.*

God's Word has no limit. We can never master
all it has to offer us.

Deuteronomy 10:14 *The highest heavens and the earth and everything in it all belong to the LORD your God.*

Psalm 50:10 *All the animals of the forest are mine, and I own the cattle on a thousand hills.* God's resources have no limit. No need is too great for him to supply.

Hebrews 7:26-28 *He is the kind of high priest we need because he is holy and blameless, unstained by sin. He has now been set apart from sinners, and he has been given the highest place of honor in heaven. He does not need to offer sacrifices every day like the other high priests. They did this for their own sins first and then for the sins of the people. But Jesus did this once for all when he sacrificed himself on the cross. Those who were high priests under the law of Moses were limited by human weakness. But after the law was given, God appointed his Son with an oath, and his Son has been made perfect forever.* God's perfection has no limit. No standard is too high for him to meet.

Psalm 103:3 *He forgives all my sins and heals all my diseases.*

Ephesians 1:7 *He is so rich in kindness that he purchased our freedom through the blood of his Son, and our sins are forgiven.*

Isaiah 1:18 *"Come now, let us argue this out,"* says the LORD. *"No matter how deep the stain of your*

sins, I can remove it. I can make you as clean as freshly fallen snow. Even if you are stained as red as crimson, I can make you as white as wool."
God's forgiveness has no limit. There is no sin too awful for him to forgive.

PROMISE FROM GOD Ephesians 3:20 *Glory be to God! By his mighty power at work within us, he is able to accomplish infinitely more than we would ever dare to ask or hope.*

Loss

How do I deal with loss in my life?
John 11:35 *Then Jesus wept.*
Don't deny your loss. Great grief is the result of great love. The tears of Jesus at Lazarus's death forever validate your tears of grief.

Genesis 50:3 *There was a period of national mourning for seventy days.*
Grief is a process that must not be denied or hurried. The rituals of wakes, visitations, funerals, and memorial services help you move through the stages of grief.

2 Samuel 11:1 *The following spring, the time of year when kings go to war, David sent Joab. . . . But David stayed behind in Jerusalem.*
For reasons not entirely known, King David gave

up the active leadership of his troops. The loss may have created a vacuum in his life that he was seeking to fill with an immoral relationship with Bathsheba. As you grieve your losses, be careful not to "medicate" your pain with that which will only create more pain.

Job 1:20-21 *Job stood up and tore his robe in grief. . . . He said, ". . . The LORD gave me everything I had, and the LORD has taken it away."*
Losses always bring pain. Recognizing and expressing your pain is not wrong or sinful, but is instead a healthy expression of how God created you.

Lamentations 3:19-23 *The thought of my suffering and homelessness is bitter beyond words. I will never forget this awful time, as I grieve over my loss. Yet I still dare to hope when I remember this: The unfailing love of the LORD never ends! By his mercies we have been kept from complete destruction. Great is his faithfulness; his mercies begin afresh each day.*
Believers grieve with God, the source of greatest hope. Unbelievers grieve without God and therefore have no hope.

Hebrews 10:34 *You suffered along with those who were thrown into jail. When all you owned was taken from you, you accepted it with joy. You knew you had better things waiting for you in eternity.*

It is important to grieve, but recognize that your grieving is short-term. One day you will be with God in heaven, where all grief will be gone forever.

I feel like I've lost everything. Where can I turn?

Psalm 31:9-10 *Have mercy on me, LORD, for I am in distress. My sight is blurred because of my tears. My body and soul are withering away. I am dying from grief; my years are shortened by sadness. Misery has drained my strength; I am wasting away from within.*

Psalm 56:8 *You keep track of all my sorrows. You have collected all my tears in your bottle. You have recorded each one in your book.*
Turn to God in times of loss, for he alone can give you hope.

Psalm 119:28 *I weep with grief; encourage me by your word.*
Turn to God's Word in times of loss, for there you will find God's wisdom.

2 Corinthians 1:4 *He comforts us in all our troubles so that we can comfort others. When others are troubled, we will be able to give them the same comfort God has given us.*
Turn to God's people in times of loss, for they can give you God's counsel.

Psalm 23:4 *Even when I walk through the dark valley of death, I will not be afraid, for you are close beside me.*
Turn to the Lord in the darkness of your grief. He promises his comfort and strength.

Isaiah 53:4 *Yet it was our weaknesses he carried; it was our sorrows that weighed him down.*
God demonstrates his love for you by being willing to experience all your griefs and sorrows.

How can God help me survive life's losses?

Psalm 10:17 *LORD, you know the hopes of the helpless. Surely you will listen to their cries and comfort them.*

2 Corinthians 1:3 *All praise to the God and Father of our Lord Jesus Christ. He is the source of every mercy and the God who comforts us.*

Matthew 5:4 *God blesses those who mourn, for they will be comforted.*

Psalm 147:3 *He heals the brokenhearted, binding up their wounds.*

Psalm 30:11-12 *You have turned my mourning into joyful dancing. You have taken away my clothes of mourning and clothed me with joy, that I might sing praises to you and not be silent. O LORD my God, I will give you thanks forever!*
In times of loss, God fills you with his blessings— comfort, joy, songs of praise, thanksgiving, and

162

mercy. When you cry out for someone to touch you, God will hold you close.

PROMISE FROM GOD Psalm 34:18
The LORD is close to the brokenhearted; he rescues those who are crushed in spirit.

Mourning

(*see also* GRIEF)

How long does mourning the loss of a loved one usually last?

Genesis 23:1-2 *When Sarah was 127 years old, she died at Kiriath-arba (now called Hebron) in the land of Canaan. There Abraham mourned and wept for her.*
You can expect that the loss of a loved one will prompt deep and difficult emotions.

Deuteronomy 34:8 *The people of Israel mourned thirty days for Moses on the plains of Moab, until the customary period of mourning was over.*
The Israelites set aside thirty days for doing nothing but mourning. Certainly their time of grief went well beyond the first month. Likewise for us, we need to take time for mourning and then expect that grief will continue with us even as we get back into our routines. Often, after the death of a spouse or parent, intense sorrow will

persist for a year or more. Don't be surprised if
it takes a long time. Remember, God walks with
you even through this dark valley.

Psalm 30:5 *Weeping may go on all night, but joy
comes with the morning.*
God's Word assures us that mourning will not
continue forever. Though you may always have
a sense of loss, the pain will eventually subside.

Revelation 21:4 *He will remove all of their
sorrows, and there will be no more death or sorrow or
crying or pain. For the old world and its evils are gone
forever.*
You can eagerly look forward to eternity, where
death and mourning will be permanently elimi-
nated.

PROMISE FROM GOD Matthew 5:4
God blesses those who mourn, for they will be comforted.

Oppression

(*see also* PERSECUTION or PREJUDICE or
SUFFERING)

What does God think of oppression?
Exodus 22:21 *Do not oppress foreigners in
any way.*
God hates oppression and expressly forbids it
in any form.

Does God care about oppressed people?

Psalm 72:12 *He will help the oppressed, who have no one to defend them.*

God has a special love for those who are oppressed; he promises to be with them and help them.

Zephaniah 3:19 *I will deal severely with all who have oppressed you.*

God promises to judge oppressors.

Luke 4:18-19 *The Spirit of the Lord is upon me, for he has appointed me to preach Good News to the poor. He has sent me to proclaim that captives will be released, that the blind will see, that the downtrodden will be freed from their oppressors, and that the time of the Lord's favor has come.*

Freeing the oppressed was a central component of Jesus' earthly ministry.

Luke 1:52 *He has taken princes from their thrones and exalted the lowly.*

When Jesus returns, he will put an end to oppression forever.

I'm only one person. What can I do about oppression?

Ezekiel 45:9 *This is what the Sovereign LORD says: Enough, you princes of Israel! Stop all your violence and oppression and do what is just and right.*

Refuse to participate in any form of oppression. Be willing, in whatever way you can, to call those in power to account.

Psalm 72:1, 4 *Give justice to the king, O God, and righteousness to the king's son. . . . Help him to defend the poor, to rescue the children of the needy, and to crush their oppressors.*
Pray that your leaders will protect the weak and punish any who oppress them. Pray for the leaders of other countries to be fair and just, and to refuse to oppress any of their people.

PROMISE FROM GOD Psalm 9:9
The LORD is a shelter for the oppressed, a refuge in times of trouble.

Overcoming

Can I really overcome the obstacles and enemies I face?

John 16:33 *Here on earth you will have many trials and sorrows. But take heart, because I have overcome the world.*
Jesus realistically prepares you for life's problems, yet he also guarantees victory.

1 John 5:4-5 *Every child of God defeats this evil world by trusting Christ to give the victory. And the ones who win this battle against the world are the ones who believe that Jesus is the Son of God.*
You overcome by trusting in Jesus' strength, not your own.

Revelation 17:14 *Together they will wage war against the Lamb, but the Lamb will defeat them because he is Lord over all lords and King over all kings, and his people are the called and chosen and faithful ones.*

When Jesus returns to rule, he will permanently overcome everything that threatens his people.

How can I overcome difficulties in my life?

Psalm 116:3-5 *Death had its hands around my throat; the terrors of the grave overtook me. I saw only trouble and sorrow. Then I called on the name of the LORD: "Please, LORD, save me!" How kind the LORD is! How good he is! So merciful, this God of ours!*

Prayer is essential to winning the victory.

2 Corinthians 4:8-9 *We are pressed on every side by troubles, but we are not crushed or broken. We are perplexed, but we don't give up and quit. We are hunted down, but God never abandons us. We get knocked down, but we get up again and keep going.*

With confidence in God's presence, you must develop the ability to endure setbacks without surrendering.

2 Corinthians 4:18 *We don't look at the troubles we can see right now; rather, we look forward to what we have not yet seen. For the troubles we see will soon be over, but the joys to come will last forever.*

An eternal perspective is an indispensable attribute

of the overcomer. Unseen solutions will replace visible problems.

PROMISE FROM GOD Romans 8:37 *No, despite all these things, overwhelming victory is ours through Christ, who loved us.*

Overwhelmed

How does God help me when I am overwhelmed?

Romans 8:35, 37-39 *Can anything ever separate us from Christ's love? Does it mean he no longer loves us if we have trouble or calamity, or are persecuted, or are hungry or cold or in danger or threatened with death? . . . No, despite all these things, overwhelming victory is ours through Christ, who loved us. And I am convinced that nothing can ever separate us from his love. Death can't, and life can't. The angels can't, and the demons can't. Our fears for today, our worries about tomorrow, and even the powers of hell can't keep God's love away. Whether we are high above the sky or in the deepest ocean, nothing in all creation will ever be able to separate us from the love of God that is revealed in Christ Jesus our Lord.*

God's love is certain, consistent, ever present, victorious. Are you feeling overwhelmed? God's love will overcome whatever overwhelms you if you let him love you.

John 14:27 *I am leaving you with a gift—peace of mind and heart. And the peace I give isn't like the peace the world gives. So don't be troubled or afraid.*
God's presence gives you peace of mind and heart in overwhelming situations. God's presence will overcome whatever overwhelms you.

Psalm 119:143 *As pressure and stress bear down on me, I find joy in your commands.*
God's Word brings deep joy and contentment in the midst of overwhelming circumstances. God's Word will overcome whatever overwhelms you.

Psalm 116:3-4 *Death had its hands around my throat; the terrors of the grave overtook me. I saw only trouble and sorrow. Then I called on the name of the LORD: "Please, LORD, save me!"*
Prayer, honestly talking and listening to God, keeps you in touch with the one whose help you need most. Prayer will overcome whatever overwhelms you.

Matthew 11:28-29 *Jesus said, "Come to me, all of you who are weary and carry heavy burdens, and I will give you rest. Take my yoke upon you. Let me teach you, because I am humble and gentle, and you will find rest for your souls."*
A healthy, growing, daily relationship with God puts overwhelming circumstances in perspective. A healthy relationship with God will overcome whatever overwhelms you.

Exodus 14:13 *Moses told the people, "Don't be afraid. Just stand where you are and watch the LORD rescue you. The Egyptians that you see today will never be seen again."*

Psalm 61:1-2 *O God, listen to my cry! Hear my prayer! From the ends of the earth, I will cry to you for help, for my heart is overwhelmed. Lead me to the towering rock of safety.*

When your troubles are overwhelming, continue to look to God and his power to help you. Bravely keep your focus on God and patiently watch him work. God's power will overcome whatever overwhelms you.

Isaiah 43:2 *When you go through deep waters and great trouble, I will be with you. When you go through rivers of difficulty, you will not drown! When you walk through the fire of oppression, you will not be burned up; the flames will not consume you.*

God loves to help those overburdened with life's troubles. He loves to pick up those who have fallen. When your life becomes overwhelming, look to him for help. God is waiting with an open hand to satisfy your need and offer strong support. God's faithfulness will overcome whatever overwhelms you.

How do I cope when life's pain becomes overwhelming?

Psalm 55:22 *Give your burdens to the LORD, and*

he will take care of you. He will not permit the godly to slip and fall.
Trust God. When you are at the bottom of life's pit, remember—the only way out is up, and God is there.

Psalm 145:14 *The LORD helps the fallen and lifts up those bent beneath their loads.*
Accept God's mercy and comfort. The Lord's arms are longer than yours, so he can always reach you in time of need.

Psalm 42:5-6 *Why am I discouraged? Why so sad? I will put my hope in God! I will praise him again—my Savior and my God!*
Hope in God. When the God of hope is near, there is no such thing as hopelessness.

Psalm 126:5-6 *Those who plant in tears will harvest with shouts of joy. They weep as they go to plant their seed, but they sing as they return with the harvest.*
Be confident of recovery, for God is good and wants to restore you.

John 16:33 *I have told you all this so that you may have peace in me. Here on earth you will have many trials and sorrows. But take heart, because I have overcome the world.*
Enjoy God's peace, for he is the only source of peace.

PROMISE FROM GOD Psalm 142:3
*I am overwhelmed, and you alone know the way
I should turn.*

Pain

How does God help me deal with my pain?

Psalm 69:16 *Answer my prayers, O LORD, for
your unfailing love is wonderful. Turn and take care
of me, for your mercy is so plentiful.*
God's unfailing love and plentiful mercy is like
medicine for your pain.

1 Peter 5:7 *Give all your worries and cares to
God, for he cares about what happens to you.*
God wants you to place your pain on his shoul-
ders, so he can bear it for you. It is easier to deal
with pain when someone is helping you through
it, and who can help you through it better than
God?

Psalm 119:76 *Now let your unfailing love
comfort me, just as you promised me, your servant.*
God comforts you in your pain with his presence
and his unfailing love.

Psalm 69:29 *I am suffering and in pain. Rescue
me, O God, by your saving power.*
God is all-powerful and can rescue you from
pain. The power of salvation will free you from
all pain in eternity.

Psalm 147:3 *He heals the brokenhearted, binding up their wounds.*
God can heal any pain, be it a broken body or a broken heart. As you wait for God's healing, either in this life or in heaven, believe that he can and will one day take it all away.

Psalm 34:18 *The LORD is close to the broken-hearted; he rescues those who are crushed in spirit.*

Isaiah 63:9 *In all their suffering he also suffered, and he personally rescued them. In his love and mercy he redeemed them. He lifted them up and carried them through all the years.*
God feels your pain. He knows what you are going through and is therefore in the best position to help you.

2 Corinthians 7:6 *But God, who encourages those who are discouraged, encouraged us by the arrival of Titus.*
God encourages you through the ministry of other believers.

What will heal my pain?
Mark 14:34-36 *He told them, "My soul is crushed with grief to the point of death. Stay here and watch with me." He went on a little farther and fell face down on the ground. He prayed that, if it were possible, the awful hour awaiting him might pass him by. "Abba, Father," he said, "everything is possible for*

*you. Please take this cup of suffering away from me.
Yet I want your will, not mine."*

Acknowledge your pain honestly to God in
prayer. Start by calling to him for help. This is
where you must begin the process of healing.

Psalm 119:28, 50, 52, 92 *I weep with grief;
encourage me by your word. . . . Your promise revives
me; it comforts me in all my troubles. . . . I meditate
on your age-old laws; O LORD, they comfort me. . . .
If your law hadn't sustained me with joy, I would
have died in my misery.*

Immerse yourself in God's Word and find
encouragement, revival, comfort, joy, and insight.

1 Peter 4:1-2 *So then, since Christ suffered
physical pain, you must arm yourselves with the same
attitude he had, and be ready to suffer, too. For if
you are willing to suffer for Christ, you have decided
to stop sinning. And you won't spend the rest of your
life chasing after evil desires, but you will be anxious
to do the will of God.*

Develop a godly perspective toward pain. This
helps you to focus less on the pain itself, which
can cause bitterness and discouragement, and
more on how this pain can help you develop
stronger character.

Proverbs 27:9 *The heartfelt counsel of a friend
is as sweet as perfume and incense.*

Seek help from godly counselors. Sometimes it is
enough to seek advice from trusted friends and

family. At other times it is necessary to talk with a trained counselor who can help you pinpoint your pain and provide effective and biblical ways to deal with it.

Romans 8:23-25 *And even we Christians, although we have the Holy Spirit within us as a fore-taste of future glory, also groan to be released from pain and suffering. We, too, wait anxiously for that day when God will give us our full rights as his children, including the new bodies he has promised us. Now that we are saved, we eagerly look forward to this freedom. For if you already have something, you don't need to hope for it. But if we look forward to something we don't have yet, we must wait patiently and confidently.*

Recognize that pain will not go on forever. In heaven, there will be no more pain.

Acts 20:37 *They wept aloud as they embraced him in farewell.*

Express your pain and don't cover it, for expression brings relief.

1 Thessalonians 3:7-8 *We have been greatly comforted, dear brothers and sisters, in all of our own crushing troubles and suffering, because you have remained strong in your faith. It gives us new life, knowing you remain strong in the Lord.*

Be encouraged by watching others who, despite their own pain, are remaining strong in their faith.

Philippians 2:4 *Don't think only about your own affairs, but be interested in others, too, and what they are doing.*
Realize that others may be hurting, too. Be sensitive to them and their pain, taking the focus off of yourself.

How is pain good for me? What can I learn from it?

Hebrews 4:15-16 *[Jesus] faced all of the same temptations we do, yet he did not sin. So let us come boldly to the throne of our gracious God. There we will receive his mercy, and we will find grace to help us when we need it.*
Pain can bring you closer to God.

2 Corinthians 12:8-10 *Three different times I begged the Lord to take it away. Each time he said, "My gracious favor is all you need. My power works best in your weakness." So now I am glad to boast about my weaknesses, so that the power of Christ may work through me. Since I know it is all for Christ's good, I am quite content with my weaknesses and with insults, hardships, persecutions, and calamities. For when I am weak, then I am strong.*
Pain can reveal God's power.

Job 6:10 *At least I can take comfort in this: Despite the pain, I have not denied the words of the Holy One.*
Pain can test and prove your commitment to God.

James 1:2-4 *Dear brothers and sisters, whenever trouble comes your way, let it be an opportunity for joy. For when your faith is tested, your endurance has a chance to grow. So let it grow, for when your endurance is fully developed, you will be strong in character and ready for anything.*

Pain can strengthen your character.

2 Corinthians 1:4, 6 *He comforts us in all our troubles so that we can comfort others. When others are troubled, we will be able to give them the same comfort God has given us. . . . So when we are weighed down with troubles, it is for your benefit and salvation! For when God comforts us, it is so that we, in turn, can be an encouragement to you. Then you can patiently endure the same things we suffer.*

Pain equips you to comfort others.

2 Corinthians 4:17 *For our present troubles are quite small and won't last very long. Yet they produce for us an immeasurably great glory that will last forever!*

Pain sparks the anticipation of the return of Jesus and your eternal life in heaven with him.

PROMISE FROM GOD 2 Corinthians 1:3 *All praise to the God and Father of our Lord Jesus Christ. He is the source of every mercy and the God who comforts us.*

Panic

What can help me when I am panicking?

Matthew 6:27-30 *Can all your worries add a single moment to your life? Of course not. And why worry about your clothes? Look at the lilies and how they grow. They don't work or make their clothing, yet Solomon in all his glory was not dressed as beautifully as they are. And if God cares so wonderfully for flowers that are here today and gone tomorrow, won't he more surely care for you?*
God's promise to take care of you.

Deuteronomy 31:7-8 *Then Moses called for Joshua, and as all Israel watched he said to him, "Be strong and courageous! For you will lead these people into the land that the LORD swore to give their ancestors. You are the one who will deliver it to them as their inheritance. Do not be afraid or discouraged, for the LORD is the one who goes before you. He will be with you; he will neither fail you nor forsake you."*
God's promise to always be by your side.

2 Timothy 3:16 *All Scripture is inspired by God and is useful to teach us what is true and to make us realize what is wrong in our lives. It straightens us out and teaches us to do what is right.*
God's promise that his Word will show you what to do.

Romans 8:27 *The Father who knows all hearts*

knows what the Spirit is saying, for the Spirit pleads for us believers in harmony with God's own will.
God's promise that his Holy Spirit prays for you.

Isaiah 26:3 *You will keep in perfect peace all who trust in you, whose thoughts are fixed on you!*
God's promise of peace of heart and mind.

Proverbs 3:26 *The LORD is your security. He will keep your foot from being caught in a trap.*
God's promise of security.

Psalm 46:1-2 *God is our refuge and strength, always ready to help in times of trouble. So we will not fear, even if earthquakes come and the mountains crumble into the sea.*
God's promise of strength just when you need it.

Luke 8:24-25 *Jesus rebuked the wind and the raging waves. The storm stopped and all was calm! Then he asked them, "Where is your faith?" And they were filled with awe and amazement. They said to one another, "Who is this man, that even the winds and waves obey him?"*
God's promise to handle any situation, to control the "uncontrollable."

How should I deal with panic? How do I find peace and perspective in the midst of panic?

Philippians 4:6-7 *Don't worry about anything; instead, pray about everything. Tell God what you need, and thank him for all he has done. If you do this, you will experience God's peace, which is far more wonderful than the human mind can understand. His peace will guard your hearts and minds as you live in Christ Jesus.*

Don't worry; pray. Worry mires you down in what you can't do. Prayer lifts you up to realize what God can do.

James 1:5 *If you need wisdom—if you want to know what God wants you to do—ask him, and he will gladly tell you. He will not resent your asking.*

Seek the Lord's guidance. Since God knows everything, it makes good sense that he knows what you should do next.

Psalm 119:95, 103-105, 165 *Though the wicked hide along the way to kill me, I will quietly keep my mind on your decrees. . . . How sweet are your words to my taste; they are sweeter than honey. Your commandments give me understanding; no wonder I hate every false way of life. Your word is a lamp for my feet and a light for my path. . . . Those who love your law have great peace and do not stumble.*

Go to God's Word. Take comfort in his promises; seek his perspective; relax in his peace.

Psalm 63:8 *I follow close behind you; your strong right hand holds me securely.*

Listen to God and follow his way. When you are certain you are following God's way, you will be calm and confident.

Psalm 112:7 *They do not fear bad news; they confidently trust the LORD to care for them.*
Act deliberately with wisdom and discretion. Understand God's perspective on life and have full confidence in him.

1 Thessalonians 5:8 *Let us who live in the light think clearly, protected by the body armor of faith and love, and wearing as our helmet the confidence of our salvation.*
Focus your thoughts clearly on God. Make sure that he is a part of each solution you are considering.

Psalm 3:5-6 *I lay down and slept. I woke up in safety, for the LORD was watching over me. I am not afraid of ten thousand enemies who surround me on every side.*
Literally, rest in the Lord. When you realize God is in control, you can sleep at night.

Psalm 131:2 *But I have stilled and quieted myself, just as a small child is quiet with its mother. Yes, like a small child is my soul within me.*
Really get to know God. To know what God says is important, to know his will is more important, but to know God personally is most important.

PROMISE FROM GOD: Isaiah 41:10 *Don't be afraid, for I am with you. Do not be dismayed, for I am your God. I will strengthen you. I will help you. I will uphold you with my victorious right hand.*

Peace

Where can I find peace?

PSALM 4:8 *I will lie down in peace and sleep, for you alone, O LORD, will keep me safe.*

PSALM 29:11 *The LORD gives his people strength. The LORD blesses them with peace.*

Peace from the chaos of the world will only come when you have entered heaven for all eternity. Peace of mind and heart come from inviting God— the true source of peace—to dwell in you, helping you to understand that this world is only temporary. Then you can navigate through any chaos because you know God is ultimately in control.

How can I get inner peace?

ROMANS 2:10 *There will be glory and honor and peace from God for all who do good.*

Turn from sin to God and live a life of obedience.

ISAIAH 26:3 *You will keep in perfect peace all who trust in you, whose thoughts are fixed on you!*

Choose to focus on the Lord more than on your problems.

PSALM 37:11 *Those who are gentle and lowly will possess the land; they will live in prosperous security.*

Humble yourself before the Lord.

PSALM 119:165 *Those who love your law have great peace and do not stumble.*

Love God's Word.

Galatians 5:22 *But when the Holy Spirit controls our lives, he will produce this kind of fruit in us: . . . peace . . .*
Let the Holy Spirit fill you and rule your life.

Philippians 4:6-7 *Don't worry about anything; instead, pray about everything. Tell God what you need, and thank him for all he has done. If you do this, you will experience God's peace, which is far more wonderful than the human mind can understand. His peace will guard your hearts and minds as you live in Christ Jesus.*
Pray about everything. Prayer is indispensable to inner peace.

Is there any hope for world peace?

Micah 4:3 *The LORD will settle international disputes. All the nations will beat their swords into plowshares and their spears into pruning hooks. All wars will stop, and military training will come to an end.*
War is an inevitable consequence of human sin. But when Jesus returns, there will be peace.

Matthew 5:9 *God blesses those who work for peace, for they will be called the children of God.*
Christians are called to work and pray for peace in the world—peace between human beings and peace between people and God. With God's help, we can make a difference!

PROMISE FROM GOD John 14:27
I am leaving you with a gift—peace of mind and heart.

Persecution

(*see also* SUFFERING)

Why are Christians persecuted?

John 15:21 *The people of the world will hate you because you belong to me, for they don't know God who sent me.*

Sometimes believers are persecuted simply for speaking the truth. Those who don't believe in God, or don't believe God has established absolute truths and communicated them through the Bible, obviously don't recognize truth. To them, truth sounds rigid and intolerant. Others recognize the truth but don't want to live by it. In either case, those who don't live by the truths of the Bible will persecute those who do.

Galatians 5:11 *The fact that I am still being persecuted proves that I am still preaching salvation.*
The bold message of Christ threatens those who believe in their own righteousness.

Where can I find hope when I am persecuted?

2 Timothy 3:12 *Everyone who wants to live a godly life in Christ Jesus will suffer persecution.*

You can be encouraged by the fact that persecution is the norm, not the exception, for faithful Christian disciples.

Acts 5:41 *The apostles left the high council rejoicing that God had counted them worthy to suffer dishonor for the name of Jesus.*
The Bible encourages you to see persecution for Jesus' sake as an honor. It is evidence of the depth of your commitment to Jesus and therefore a privilege to suffer for the God you love so much. It also acknowledges the depth of suffering Jesus went through for us.

Matthew 5:11 *God blesses you when you are mocked and persecuted and lied about because you are my followers.*
Jesus promises special blessings to those who are persecuted for his sake.

Psalm 110:1 *The LORD said to my Lord, "Sit in honor at my right hand, until I humble your enemies, making them a footstool under your feet."*
God will defeat his enemies. You may be persecuted now, but you will ultimately rejoice in God's victory.

As a Christian, how should I respond when I am persecuted for my faith?
Psalm 69:1, 4 *Save me, O God. . . . Those who hate me without cause are more numerous than the hairs on my head.*

Turn to prayer in times of persecution. Only God can give you the strength to endure.

Acts 14:19-20 *They stoned Paul and dragged him out of the city, apparently dead. But as the believers stood around him, he got up and went back into the city.* Paul's courageous response to persecution enabled him to encourage others. Courage to endure persecution is contagious.

Revelation 21:4 *He will remove all of their sorrows.* The hope that all suffering will be replaced by the joy of heaven will help you to endure.

2 Thessalonians 1:5 *But God will use this persecution to show his justice. For he will make you worthy of his Kingdom, for which you are suffering.* Be aware that God will use persecution to build your character and faith.

Romans 12:14 *If people persecute you because you are a Christian, don't curse them; pray that God will bless them.* Pray that God will bless those who persecute you, for it may be through your godly response to their persecution that God touches a hard heart and turns it to him.

Revelation 14:12 *Let this encourage God's holy people to endure persecution patiently and remain firm to the end, obeying his commands and trusting in Jesus.*

Remain obedient to God and endure the persecution patiently, just as Jesus did when he was persecuted.

PROMISE FROM GOD Revelation 2:10 *Don't be afraid of what you are about to suffer. . . . Remain faithful even when facing death, and I will give you the crown of life.*

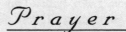

What is prayer?

2 Chronicles 7:14 *If my people who are called by my name will humble themselves and pray and seek my face and turn from their wicked ways, I will hear from heaven.*

Prayer is an act of humble worship in which you seek God with all your heart. The simplicity of prayer is conversation with the Lord. The majesty of prayer is to humbly enter the very presence of almighty God.

1 John 1:9 *If we confess our sins to him, he is faithful and just to forgive us and to cleanse us from every wrong.*

Prayer often begins with confession of sin. It is through confession that you find forgiveness.

1 Samuel 14:36 *The priest said, "Let's ask God first."*

187

Prayer is asking God for guidance and waiting for his direction and leading.

Mark 1:35 *The next morning Jesus awoke long before daybreak and went out alone into the wilderness to pray.*

Prayer is an expression of an intimate relationship with your heavenly Father, who makes his love and resources available to you.

Psalm 9:1-2 *I will thank you, LORD, with all my heart. . . . I will sing praises to your name, O Most High.*

Through prayer you praise your mighty God.

Does God always answer prayer?

Psalm 116:1-2 *I love the LORD because he hears and answers my prayers. Because he bends down and listens, I will pray as long as I have breath!*

God always listens and responds to our prayers. But, as our loving heavenly Father who knows what is best, he does not always give us what we ask for. He answers, but sometimes that answer is no.

2 Corinthians 12:8-9 *Three different times I begged the Lord to take it away. Each time he said, ". . . My power works best in your weakness."*

Sometimes, like Paul, you will find that God answers prayer by giving you not what you ask for but something better.

1 John 5:14 We can be confident that he will listen to us whenever we ask him for anything in line with his will.
As you maintain a close relationship with Jesus and his Word, your prayers will align with his will. When that happens, God is delighted to grant your requests.

John 14:14 Ask anything in my name, and I will do it!
Praying in Jesus' name means praying according to Jesus' character and purposes. When you pray like this, you are asking for what God already wants to give you.

Exodus 14:15 The LORD said to Moses, "Why are you crying out to me? Tell the people to get moving!"
Effective prayer is accompanied by a willingness to obey. When God opens a door, you must walk through it.

PROMISE FROM GOD James 5:16
The earnest prayer of a righteous person has great power and wonderful results.

Prejudice

What does God think of prejudice?
John 4:9 The woman was surprised, for Jews refuse to have anything to do with Samaritans. She

said to Jesus, "You are a Jew, and I am a Samaritan woman. Why are you asking me for a drink?"
Jesus reached across lines of racial prejudice and division.

Acts 10:28 Peter told them, "You know it is against the Jewish laws for me to come into a Gentile home like this. But God has shown me that I should never think of anyone as impure."
God wants us to overcome our racial prejudices. All the things of God are available equally to all people.

What kind of prejudice does God condemn?

1 Samuel 16:7 Don't judge by his appearance or height. . . . The LORD doesn't make decisions the way you do! People judge by outward appearance, but the LORD looks at a person's thoughts and intentions.
God condemns prejudice based on outward appearance. Stereotypes abound—prejudice against fat people, short people, skinny people, ugly people, black people, white people, yellow people, people with skin defects, bald people—the list goes on. But the real person is inside; the body is only the shell, the temporary housing. It is wrong to judge a person by the outward appearance; the real person inside may be quite different from how they appear. Even Jesus may not have had the tall, handsome body often attributed to him, for Isaiah the prophet said

about the coming Savior, "There was nothing beautiful or majestic about his appearance" (Isaiah 53:2).

Esther 3:5-6 *[Haman] was filled with rage. So he decided it was not enough to lay hands on Mordecai alone. . . . He decided to destroy all the Jews throughout the entire empire.*
The Bible encourages us not to form an opinion about an entire group of people (nationality, church denomination, local club) based on the actions of one individual.

Proverbs 14:31 *Those who oppress the poor insult their Maker, but those who help the poor honor him.*

James 2:9 *But if you pay special attention to the rich, you are committing a sin.*
God condemns prejudice based on financial well-being or socioeconomic class. Money is not a measure of character.

1 Timothy 4:12 *Don't let anyone think less of you because you are young.*

1 Timothy 5:1 *Never speak harshly to an older man, but appeal to him respectfully as though he were your own father. Talk to the younger men as you would to your own brothers.*
The Bible forbids discrimination based on age. Maturity is not always a by-product of age.

M a r k 6 : 2 - 3 *Where did he get all his wisdom and the power to perform such miracles? He's just the carpenter, the son of Mary.*
God does not write off families or occupations, and perhaps that is why Jesus was born as the son of a carpenter rather than the son of a king. God loves each person, regardless of occupation.

A c t s 1 0 : 2 8 *Peter told them, "You know it is against the Jewish laws for me to come into a Gentile home like this. But God has shown me that I should never think of anyone as impure."*

A c t s 1 0 : 3 4 - 3 5 *Then Peter replied, "I see very clearly that God doesn't show partiality. In every nation he accepts those who fear him and do what is right."*
God condemns racial prejudice. In heaven there are no ethnic groups, no races, no distinctions such as these, so why should they be important now?

J o h n 1 : 4 6 *"Nazareth!" exclaimed Nathanael. "Can anything good come from there?"*
We must not be prejudiced because of the place where a person grew up. The "other side of the tracks" is often viewed negatively, but God lives on both sides of the tracks.

P R O M I S E F R O M G O D G a l a t i a n s 3 : 2 8 *There is no longer Jew or Gentile, slave or free, male or female. For you are all Christians— you are one in Christ Jesus.*

Presence of God

How can I experience God's presence for today on earth and for eternity in heaven?

James 4:8 *Draw close to God, and God will draw close to you. Wash your hands, you sinners; purify your hearts, you hypocrites.*

God is with you everywhere, and you can draw near to him at any time.

Revelation 3:20 *Look! Here I stand at the door and knock. If you hear me calling and open the door, I will come in, and we will share a meal as friends.*

You must believe that he is, before you can believe that he is with you.

Matthew 18:3 *Then he said, "I assure you, unless you turn from your sins and become as little children, you will never get into the Kingdom of Heaven."*

There is only one way to experience God's eternal presence—to turn from your sins, ask God to forgive your sins, and ask Jesus to be Lord of your life.

John 14:23 *Jesus replied, "All those who love me will do what I say. My Father will love them, and we will come to them and live with them."*

God longs for you to enjoy fellowship with him. God's solution to the sin in your life is for you to come to him through believing and accepting

Jesus' payment for your sin, turning from your sin, and obeying God. You experience God's presence daily as you look to him and obey him.

How can I be assured of God's presence?

P s a l m 1 3 9 : 5 , 7 *You both precede and follow me. You place your hand of blessing on my head. . . . I can never escape from your spirit! I can never get away from your presence!*
His presence is always with you. Nothing can separate you from his love for you.

P s a l m 1 6 : 8 *I know the LORD is always with me. I will not be shaken, for he is right beside me.*
God's presence is with you regardless of life's circumstances.

What should I do when it feels like God is far away?

P s a l m 1 3 9 : 7 *I can never escape from your spirit! I can never get away from your presence!*
God will go to any height or depth to be with you—he is always by your side. Don't trust your feelings; trust God's promises.

J o b 2 3 : 8 *I go east. . . . I go west, but I cannot find him.*
Faith is trusting, even when you feel far from God. When you cannot find him, wait expectantly—he knows where you are.

PROMISE FROM GOD Isaiah 46:4
I will be your God throughout your lifetime—until your hair is white with age. I made you, and I will care for you. I will carry you along and save you.

Problems

(*see also* ADVERSITY)

How does God view my problems?

1 Peter 5:7 *Give all your worries and cares to God, for he cares about what happens to you.*
God cares about you and your problems.

Psalm 145:14 *The LORD helps the fallen and lifts up those bent beneath their loads.*
God is not only aware of your problems, he wants to help you solve them.

Exodus 4:10-12 *But Moses pleaded with the LORD, "O Lord, I'm just not a good speaker. I never have been, and I'm not now, even after you have spoken to me. I'm clumsy with words." "Who makes mouths?" the LORD asked him. "Who makes people so they can speak or not speak, hear or not hear, see or not see? Is it not I, the LORD? Now go, and do as I have told you. I will help you speak well, and I will tell you what to say."*
God specifically addresses your problems with trustworthy, sure solutions. If you take your

problems to God, expect him to deal with them, but expect that he will deal with them his way, which is always in your best interest.

Acts 8:4 *But the believers who had fled Jerusalem went everywhere preaching the Good News about Jesus.*
God may use your problems to give you unexpected assignments.

How can I anticipate problems and prepare for them?

James 1:2 *Dear brothers and sisters, whenever trouble comes your way, let it be an opportunity for joy.*
Realize that problems are inevitable; they will come. So the question is not, "Will problems come?" but "What will I do with problems when they come?"

Ephesians 6:11-12 *Put on all of God's armor so that you will be able to stand firm against all strategies and tricks of the Devil. For we are not fighting against people made of flesh and blood, but against the evil rulers and authorities of the unseen world, against those mighty powers of darkness who rule this world, and against wicked spirits in the heavenly realms.*
Living a life of faith, love, obedience, and prayer prepares you for life's inevitable problems. You are encouraged to be strong with God's power. If you go onto life's battlefields already equipped with God's spiritual armor, you will more quickly

and easily win the battles that your problems bring.

How can I best cope with life's problems?

Psalm 56:3-4 *But when I am afraid, I put my trust in you. O God, I praise your word. I trust in God, so why should I be afraid? What can mere mortals do to me?*

Make God your primary point of confidence. At times your problems are just too big for you, so you need someone bigger, wiser, and stronger than you or your problems to help, and that is God. Communicate with him honestly about your worries and fears.

Psalm 119:24 *Your decrees please me; they give me wise advice.*

God's Word is the best source of wise counsel.

Mark 5:36 *But Jesus ignored their comments and said to Jairus, "Don't be afraid. Just trust me."*

Seeking God's solutions for your problems can enhance your faith, praise, and joy.

How should I learn and grow from my problems?

Psalm 107:43 *Those who are wise will take all this to heart; they will see in our history the faithful love of the LORD.*

The more you see God at work in your problems, the more you learn about his faithful, loving character in your life. The more you learn about what God does, the more you will want to learn about who he is.

Romans 5:3-4 *We can rejoice, too, when we run into problems and trials, for we know that they are good for us—they help us learn to endure. And endurance develops strength of character in us, and character strengthens our confident expectation of salvation.* The more you endure life's problems, the more you see your own character strengthened. The more you become the kind of person God desires, the more you can do the kind of work God desires.

2 Corinthians 6:3-4 *We try to live in such a way that no one will be hindered from finding the Lord by the way we act, and so no one can find fault with our ministry. In everything we do we try to show that we are true ministers of God.* The more you endure life's problems, the more you learn what is most important in life. The more you realize what is most important, the more you will put first things first.

2 Corinthians 1:8-9 *We were crushed and completely overwhelmed, and we thought we would never live through it. In fact, we expected to die. But as a result, we learned not to rely on ourselves, but on God who can raise the dead.* The more you endure life's problems, the more you learn the source of your strength and your help. When you realize the source of your strength, you should have the good sense to go to that source of strength.

How can I help others in the midst of their problems?

1 Peter 4:8 *Most important of all, continue to show deep love for each other, for love covers a multitude of sins.*

You can genuinely love others with your actions, your emotions, your attitudes, your words, and your presence. Love resolves a thousand problems and prevents a thousand more.

PROMISE FROM GOD Philippians 4:6 *Don't worry about anything; instead, pray about everything. Tell God what you need, and thank him for all he has done.*

$\mathcal{P}$*romises*

Are God's promises really trustworthy?

Numbers 23:19 *God is not a man, that he should lie. He is not a human, that he should change his mind. Has he ever spoken and failed to act? Has he ever promised and not carried it through?*

God's promises are completely trustworthy—they rest on his unchanging character! The promises from a perfect God cannot fail.

Why does it sometimes seem as if God hasn't fulfilled his promises?

2 Peter 3:8 *You must not forget, dear friends, that a day is like a thousand years to the Lord, and a thousand years is like a day.*

Habakkuk 2:3 *These things I plan won't happen right away. Slowly, steadily, surely, the time approaches when the vision will be fulfilled. If it seems slow, wait patiently, for it will surely take place. It will not be delayed.*

God will fulfill his promises, but sometimes his timetable is different from ours. You may sometimes feel like there are so many things God could and should be doing according to all that he has promised. Wait and trust, confident in God's truthfulness. He will completely fulfill every promise.

How should God's promises impact my life?

Hebrews 6:18 *So God has given us both his promise and his oath. These two things are unchangeable because it is impossible for God to lie. Therefore, we who have fled to him for refuge can take new courage, for we can hold on to his promise with confidence.*

The trustworthiness of God gives great comfort in the present and assurance for the future. When you are absolutely convinced that God is able to do anything he promises, then the troubles of this world are put in perspective.

2 Corinthians 7:1 *Because we have these promises, dear friends, let us cleanse ourselves from everything that can defile our body or spirit. And let us work toward complete purity because we fear God.* God's promises should prompt you to obedience. The promise of Christ's imminent return is also a great motivation for Christian conduct!

Luke 1:12-13 *Zechariah was overwhelmed with fear. But the angel said, "Don't be afraid, Zechariah! For God has heard your prayer, and your wife, Elizabeth, will bear you a son! And you are to name him John."* As soon as God promises something, fear becomes unnecessary. You should not fear uncertainty over what God has promised, for when God promises, it is no longer uncertain.

Hebrews 11:13 *All these faithful ones died without receiving what God had promised them, but they saw it all from a distance and welcomed the promises of God.* Great people of God died without seeing God's promises fulfilled. Faith in God's promises does not require that you see all his promises fulfilled in your lifetime. God's promises are sometimes fulfilled in heaven not earth, but each one of his promises will be fulfilled in his perfect timing.

With so little to depend on in life, what can I count on from God?

Galatians 3:22 *The only way to receive God's promise is to believe in Jesus Christ.*
God's promises apply to his children, those who have received his offer of salvation through faith. If you want to know that you can count on God, then you need to receive Jesus Christ as your personal Savior.

Ephesians 1:14 *The Spirit is God's guarantee that he will give us everything he promised.*
You can count on getting everything God has promised because of the Holy Spirit's presence in your life. The Holy Spirit is God's guarantee that his promises are trustworthy.

John 14:2 *I am going to prepare a place for you. If this were not so, I would tell you plainly.*
You can count on having an eternal home in heaven, for Jesus said it plainly.

John 14:16-17 *And I will ask the Father, and he will give you another Counselor, who will never leave you. He is the Holy Spirit.*
You can count on the presence of Jesus with you forever in the form of the Holy Spirit.

2 Peter 3:10 *The day of the Lord will come.*
You can count on the fact that Jesus will return to judge the world.

Romans 8:28 *We know that God causes every-thing to work together for the good of those who love God and are called according to his purpose for them.* You can count on the truth that all of the events of your life will work together for your good.

Hebrews 6:18 *God has given us both his promise and his oath. These two things are unchangeable because it is impossible for God to lie.* You can count on God's promises as completely dependable and trustworthy because God himself is so. This should give you great comfort in the present and assurance for the future. If the past and present verify God's dependability, the future will certainly anticipate his continued depend-ability.

PROMISE FROM GOD Hebrews 10:23 *Without wavering, let us hold tightly to the hope we say we have, for God can be trusted to keep his promise.*

Protection

Does God promise to protect me?
Daniel 3:17-18 *The God whom we serve is able to save us. . . . but even if he doesn't . . .* God promises to protect and keep safe those who love him. But the ultimate fulfillment of this

promise is in the spiritual protection of God's loving grace rather than physical protection. Christians will be saved from eternal destruction. Like Daniel's friends, you must commit yourself to obeying God no matter what happens to your earthly body.

Psalm 17:8, 15 *Guard me as the apple of your eye. . . . When I awake, I will be fully satisfied, for I will see you face to face.*
The psalmist prayed to God for protection from his enemies, yet trusted that ultimate safety is God's salvation, which leads to the hope of heaven.

Philippians 4:7 *His peace will guard your hearts and minds as you live in Christ Jesus.*
Through consistent and devoted prayer, you can know the protection of God's supernatural peace.

Jeremiah 42:13, 16 *But if you refuse to obey the LORD . . . the war and famine you fear will follow close behind you.*
Jeremiah teaches the relationship between obedience and the protection of God. Obedience to God will protect you from the consequences of disobedience. For example, obeying God's command not to cheat will protect you from the embarrassment, loss of friendships, fines, and potential jail time that can come from cheating.

PROMISE FROM GOD Psalm 91:11
For he orders his angels to protect you wherever you go.

Provision

What does it mean to trust God's provision? Can I really trust him to take care of me?

Joshua 3:9-10 *Come and listen to what the LORD your God says. Today you will know that the living God is among you.*

You can trust him to care for you if you are being obedient to him.

Exodus 16:4, 19-20 *Then the LORD said to Moses, "Look, I am going to rain down food from heaven for you. . . . Then Moses told [the people], "Do not keep any of it overnight." But, of course, some of them didn't listen and kept some of it until morning. By then it was full of maggots.*

You can trust him to care for your physical needs when you are willing to recognize his care and be thankful. Too often, people trust God for provision, but then think that he hasn't provided because they didn't get everything they desired.

2 Peter 1:3 *As we know Jesus better, his divine power gives us everything we need for living a godly life.*

You can trust him to care for your spiritual needs. God has provided resources from his own character to those who seek him.

John 6:35 *Jesus replied, "I am the bread of life. No one who comes to me will ever be hungry again."*

205

You can trust him to fill your deepest hunger. God knows that what you really need is to have your heart filled with the love and power of Christ himself.

PROMISE FROM GOD Philippians 4:19 *This same God who takes care of me will supply all your needs from his glorious riches, which have been given to us in Christ Jesus.*

Quitting

(*see also* ENDURANCE)

How can I keep going when I feel like quitting?

Nehemiah 4:2-3 *What does this bunch of poor, feeble Jews think they are doing? . . . That stone wall would collapse if even a fox walked along the top of it!* Faced with an overwhelming task and ridicule from adversaries, Nehemiah kept his eyes on the goal and his call. You reach your goal when you keep yourself focused on it.

Acts 20:22 *And now I am going to Jerusalem, drawn there irresistibly by the Holy Spirit, not knowing what awaits me.*
Paul faced unimaginable hardship yet never gave up, finishing the work to which God had called him. Most people can begin a good work, but it takes spiritual strength from Christ to finish well.

206

2 Corinthians 4:8 *We are pressed on every side by troubles, but we are not crushed and broken. We are perplexed, but we don't give up and quit.* Even in the midst of suffering, you can find strength to endure for Christ.

2 Timothy 4:7 *I have fought a good fight, I have finished the race, and I have remained faithful.*

Galatians 6:9 *Don't get tired of doing what is good. Don't get discouraged and give up, for we will reap a harvest of blessing at the appropriate time.* You can avoid discouragement and the desire to quit by keeping your eyes on the goal and reward of heaven.

PROMISE FROM GOD Matthew 10:22 *And everyone will hate you because of your allegiance to me. But those who endure to the end will be saved.*

Renewal

My life is such a mess. I'm confused. I really feel the need to begin again. How can I experience renewal in my life?

Acts 3:19 *Now turn from your sins and turn to God, so you can be cleansed of your sins.*

Ezekiel 36:26-27 *And I will give you a new heart with new and right desires, and I will put a new*

207

spirit in you. I will take out your stony heart of sin and give you a new, obedient heart. And I will put my Spirit in you so you will obey my laws and do whatever I command.

Ephesians 4:22-24 *Throw off your old evil nature and your former way of life, which is rotten through and through. . . . Instead, there must be a spiritual renewal of your thoughts and attitudes. You must display a new nature because you are a new person, created in God's likeness—righteous, holy, and true.*

Colossians 3:10 *In its place you have clothed yourselves with a brand-new nature that is continually being renewed as you learn more and more about Christ, who created this new nature within you.*
Do you want renewal? Then turn to God, confess your sins, and let him cleanse your heart and life. He promises to make you a brand new person!

In what ways does God renew me?
Psalm 19:7 *The law of the LORD is perfect, reviving the soul. The decrees of the LORD are trustworthy, making wise the simple.*
God revives your soul.

Psalm 119:25 *I lie in the dust, completely discouraged; revive me by your word.*
God revives you by his Word.

Psalm 23:3 *He renews my strength. He guides me along right paths, bringing honor to his name.*

God renews your strength and promises to guide you on new pathways for your life.

Psalm 94:19 *When doubts filled my mind, your comfort gave me renewed hope and cheer.*
God renews your hope.

Psalm 119:40, 93 *I long to obey your commandments! Renew my life with your goodness. . . . I will never forget your commandments, for you have used them to restore my joy and health.*
God restores your joy and health.

2 Corinthians 4:16 *That is why we never give up. Though our bodies are dying, our spirits are being renewed every day.*
God renews your spirit.

PROMISE FROM GOD Psalm 51:10 *Create in me a clean heart, O God. Renew a right spirit within me.*

Rescue

From what does God rescue me?

Romans 5:6 *When we were utterly helpless, Christ came at just the right time and died for us sinners.*

Galatians 1:4 *He died for our sins, just as God our Father planned, in order to rescue us from this evil world in which we live.*

God rescues you from the pain and eternal consequences of sin. Now you are free from the hurt that comes from sin and you can experience the joy and freedom of a relationship with the eternal God.

Revelation 1:5 *All praise to him who loves us and has freed us from our sins by shedding his blood for us.*

2 Corinthians 3:17 *Now, the Lord is the Spirit, and wherever the Spirit of the Lord is, he gives freedom.*
God rescues you from the power of sin. When you are rescued, you are free to serve God and others in love.

Colossians 1:13-14 *He has rescued us from the one who rules in the kingdom of darkness, and he has brought us into the Kingdom of his dear Son. God has purchased our freedom with his blood and has forgiven all our sins.*

Luke 11:21-22 *When Satan, who is completely armed, guards his palace, it is safe—until someone who is stronger attacks and overpowers him, strips him of his weapons, and carries off his belongings.*
God rescues you from the dominion of Satan. You are no longer a slave to sin, bound by the control of Satan and his temptations. You are free to live as God wants you to live. Satan no longer has control over you.

Psalm 34:4 *I prayed to the LORD, and he answered me, freeing me from all my fears.*

Hebrews 2:14-15 *Because God's children are human beings—made of flesh and blood—Jesus also became flesh and blood by being born in human form. For only as a human being could he die, and only by dying could he break the power of the Devil, who had the power of death. Only in this way could he deliver those who have lived all their lives as slaves to the fear of dying.*

God rescues you from fear, even the fear of death.

Daniel 6:27 *He rescues and saves his people; he performs miraculous signs and wonders in the heavens and on earth. He has rescued Daniel from the power of the lions.*

Psalm 91:14-15 *The LORD says, "I will rescue those who love me. I will protect those who trust in my name. When they call on me, I will answer; I will be with them in trouble. I will rescue them and honor them."*

God rescues you in your times of trouble. He does not always prevent or remove the trouble, but he is always present in troubled times. Moreover, he is able to use your troubles for his glory.

Psalm 72:12-14 *He will rescue the poor when they cry to him; he will help the oppressed, who have no one to defend them. He feels pity for the weak and the needy, and he will rescue them. He will save them*

211

*from oppression and from violence, for their lives are
precious to him.*
God rescues you from oppression.

1 Corinthians 10:13 *Remember that the
temptations that come into your life are no different
from what others experience. And God is faithful. He
will keep the temptation from becoming so strong that
you can't stand up against it. When you are tempted,
he will show you a way out so that you will not give
in to it.*
God rescues you from temptations. He does not
always remove the temptations, but gives you the
resources to be victorious over them.

How does God rescue me?

Psalm 142:1-7 *I cry out to the LORD; I plead
for the LORD's mercy. I pour out my complaints
before him and tell him all my troubles. For I am
overwhelmed, and you alone know the way I should
turn. Wherever I go, my enemies have set traps for
me. I look for someone to come and help me, but no
one gives me a passing thought! No one will help me;
no one cares a bit what happens to me. Then I pray
to you, O LORD. I say, "You are my place of refuge.
You are all I really want in life. Hear my cry, for
I am very low. Rescue me from my persecutors, for
they are too strong for me. Bring me out of prison so
I can thank you. The godly will crowd around me,
for you treat me kindly."*

God rescues you by guiding you along the right path of life. Because of his love for you and his mercy toward you, he brings you close to him, where you cannot be defeated by your enemies.

Micah 7:15 *"Yes," says the LORD, "I will do mighty miracles for you, like those I did when I rescued you from slavery in Egypt."*

Acts 12:7, 11 *Suddenly, there was a bright light in the cell, and an angel of the Lord stood before Peter. The angel tapped him on the side to awaken him and said, "Quick! Get up!" And the chains fell off his wrists. . . . Peter finally realized what had happened. "It's really true!" he said to himself. "The Lord has sent his angel and saved me from Herod and from what the Jews were hoping to do to me!"*
God rescues you with miracles. Sometimes there is no way out of trouble except for God to miraculously intervene on your behalf.

2 Corinthians 1:11 *He will rescue us because you are helping by praying for us. As a result, many will give thanks to God because so many people's prayers for our safety have been answered.*
God often rescues you with the help of people—believers and unbelievers—as his agents of rescue on your behalf.

Why doesn't God rescue me from all my troubles?

Daniel 3:17-18 *If we are thrown into the*

blazing furnace, the God whom we serve is able to save us. He will rescue us from your power, Your Majesty. But even if he doesn't, Your Majesty can be sure that we will never serve your gods or worship the gold statue you have set up.

Matthew 26:53-54 *Don't you realize that I could ask my Father for thousands of angels to protect us, and he would send them instantly? But if I did, how would the Scriptures be fulfilled that describe what must happen now?*

2 Timothy 4:18 *Yes, and the Lord will deliver me from every evil attack and will bring me safely to his heavenly Kingdom. To God be the glory forever and ever.*

Knowing God does not exempt you from troubles here on earth. But God is clearly able to give you the strength and wisdom to overcome any and every trouble. He lovingly and sovereignly determines the timing and details of your rescue. All believers will eventually be rescued from all earthly troubles to live with him trouble free forever.

PROMISE FROM GOD Psalm 18:19 *He led me to a place of safety; he rescued me because he delights in me.*

Safety

(*see also* PROTECTION)

Will God keep me safe from physical harm?

Daniel 6:22 *My God sent his angel to shut the lions' mouths so that they would not hurt me.*

Psalm 91:11 *For he orders his angels to protect you wherever you go.*

Sometimes God protects and delivers in miraculous ways in order to preserve you so you can continue to serve him.

2 Corinthians 12:7 *I was given a thorn in my flesh, a messenger from Satan to torment me and keep me from getting proud.*

At other times even God's chosen servants experience devastating physical hardship and suffering. These are the times when your faith is put to the test. At those times, don't lose your eternal perspective.

Romans 5:3 *We can rejoice, too, when we run into problems and trials.*

When God does not prevent suffering, he promises strength to endure through the Holy Spirit. Enduring suffering may bring you closer to God than being spared from suffering.

Deuteronomy 30:20 *Choose to love the LORD your God and to obey him. . . . Then you will live long in the land.*

Through his Word, God offers wisdom that helps you avoid needless peril.

If God doesn't guarantee physical safety, what's the point of faith?

John 17:16 *They are not part of this world any more than I am.*
Faith has more to do with the eternal safety of your soul than the physical safety of your body.

2 Timothy 1:12 *I know the one in whom I trust, and I am sure that he is able to guard what I have entrusted to him until the day of his return.*
Faith is trusting God to guard and keep that which is eternal—your soul.

1 Peter 2:25 *Now you have turned to your Shepherd, the Guardian of your souls.*
Christ, the shepherd of your soul, guards you from the enemy's attacks.

1 Peter 3:18 *He died for sinners that he might bring us safely home to God.*
Faith in Christ gives you safe passage to your eternal home.

Is it wrong to pray for safety for myself and my loved ones?

Acts 12:5 *While Peter was in prison, the church prayed very earnestly for him.*
God always welcomes the confession of your desires when offered in submission to his will.

Romans 1:10 *One of the things I always pray for is the opportunity, God willing, to come at last to see you.*
Paul's desire for safety in travel was rooted in his desire to minister to others.

2 Corinthians 1:11 *He will rescue us because you are helping by praying for us.*
The early apostles depended on the prayers for safety offered by the churches.

PROMISE FROM GOD Psalm 34:7
The angel of the LORD guards all who fear him, and he rescues them.

Salvation

What does it mean to be saved?
Romans 4:8 *What joy for those whose sin is no longer counted against them by the Lord.*

Romans 3:24 *Yet now God in his gracious kindness declares us not guilty.*
Being saved means no longer having your sins count against you. You have been forgiven by the grace of God. Being saved does not spare you from earthly troubles, but it does spare you from eternal judgment.

Psalm 103:12 *He has removed our rebellious acts as far away from us as the east is from the west.*

Being saved means your sins have been completely removed.

Psalm 51:9-10 *Remove the stain of my guilt. Create in me a clean heart, O God.*
Being saved means the stain of your guilt has been washed away. It not only appears to be gone, it is gone!

John 5:24 *I assure you, those who listen to my message and believe in God who sent me have eternal life.*
Being saved means you are forgiven in Christ and are assured of eternal life in heaven. What greater hope could you have?

How can I be saved?
Romans 10:13 *Anyone who calls on the name of the Lord will be saved.*
You can be saved by calling on the name of the Lord. Call out to him in prayer and tell him that you want him to save you. He will. He promises.

John 3:16 *For God so loved the world that he gave his only Son, so that everyone who believes in him will not perish but have eternal life.*

Acts 16:31 *Believe on the Lord Jesus and you will be saved.*
You can be saved by believing that the Lord Jesus died to save you from your sins and rose again to give you eternal life.

PROMISE FROM GOD Romans
10:9 *If you confess with your mouth that Jesus is Lord and believe in your heart that God raised him from the dead, you will be saved.*

Security

(*see also* PROTECTION or SAFETY or SALVATION)

With so much change and instability in the world, how does my faith bring security?

Psalm 125:1 *Those who trust in the LORD are as secure as Mount Zion; they will not be defeated but will endure forever.*

Proverbs 1:33 *But all who listen to me will live in peace and safety, unafraid of harm.*
When you build your life on God's truth, you have a solid foundation that will not crack under the world's pressure. The Christian's safety and security is rooted deeply in the Lord's presence. With him you can face life with great courage; without him you stand alone.

How does God provide security?

Proverbs 14:26 *Those who fear the LORD are secure; he will be a place of refuge for their children.*

Psalm 63:8 *I follow close behind you; your strong right hand holds me securely.*

No matter how much the storms of life batter you, you are eternally secure with God. Nothing can ever separate you from his eternal presence.

How can I feel secure about the future?

Philippians 4:6-7 *Don't worry about anything; instead, pray about everything. . . . If you do this, you will experience God's peace, which is far more wonderful than the human mind can understand.*
Your greatest security comes from knowing the peace of God through prayer.

Romans 8:39 *Nothing in all creation will ever be able to separate us from the love of God.*
The most powerful security in the world is knowing that nothing can separate you from the love of God.

1 John 5:18 *We know that those who have become part of God's family do not make a practice of sinning, for God's Son holds them securely, and the evil one cannot get his hands on them.*

1 Peter 1:4-5 *For God has reserved a priceless inheritance for his children. It is kept in heaven for you, pure and undefiled, beyond the reach of change and decay. And God, in his mighty power, will protect you until you receive this salvation, because you are trusting him. It will be revealed on the last day for all to see.*
God has promised to save you when you accept his Son, Jesus Christ, as your Savior. God always

keeps his promises. When Jesus holds you securely, Satan cannot get his hands on you.

PROMISE FROM GOD Revelation 3 : 5 *All who are victorious will be clothed in white. I will never erase their names from the Book of Life, but I will announce before my Father and his angels that they are mine.*

Sorrow

(*see also* ENCOURAGEMENT)

I have trouble reconciling the sorrow and grief of life with the love of God. Is God concerned about my pain?
Isaiah 53:3 *He was despised and rejected— a man of sorrows.*
Through the pain and sorrow of Christ's experiences on earth, God has experienced the depths of human grief.

John 11:35-36 *Then Jesus wept. The people who were standing nearby said, "See how much he loved him."*
The tears of Jesus demonstrate that great grief comes from great love.

Luke 19:41 *But as they came closer to Jerusalem and Jesus saw the city ahead, he began to cry.*

221

Jesus grieves when those he loves do not respond to his offer of salvation.

1 Peter 5:7 *Give all your worries and cares to God, for he cares about what happens to you.*
God cares not only about your eternal future, but also about your present troubles.

How can I find hope in my times of sorrow?

Psalm 30:5 *Weeping may go on all night, but joy comes with the morning.*

Revelation 21:4 *He will remove all of their sorrows, and there will be no more death or sorrow or crying or pain.*
God promises to relieve your weeping and replace it with his joy.

1 Thessalonians 4:13 *I want you to know what will happen to the Christians who have died so you will not be full of sorrow like people who have no hope.*
Your grief can be filled with hope through the promise of heaven.

Romans 8:26 *The Holy Spirit prays for us with groanings that cannot be expressed in words.*
Even when you don't know what to pray, the Holy Spirit prays for you.

Romans 12:15 *If they are sad, share their sorrow.*

2 Corinthians 1:4 *He comforts us in all our troubles so that we can comfort others.*
After you have received the comfort of Christ in the midst of your grief, you become a comforting presence to others.

PROMISE FROM GOD Isaiah 25:8
He will swallow up death forever! The Sovereign LORD will wipe away all tears.

Strength

How do I really know that God is strong? With what's going on in the world, it doesn't look as though he's very strong at all.

Psalm 104:1-3,32 *O LORD my God, how great you are! . . . You stretch out the starry curtain of the heavens; you lay out the rafters of your home in the rain clouds. You make the clouds your chariots; you ride upon the wings of the wind. . . . The earth trembles at his glance; the mountains burst into flame at his touch.*

Jeremiah 32:17 *O Sovereign LORD! You have made the heavens and earth by your great power. Nothing is too hard for you!*
God created and sustains the universe as evidence of his mighty power. There is no greater strength.

Psalm 135:6 *The LORD does whatever pleases him throughout all heaven and earth, and on the seas and in their depths.*

Psalm 46:8-10 *Come, see the glorious works of the LORD: See how he brings destruction upon the world and causes wars to end throughout the earth. He breaks the bow and snaps the spear in two; he burns the shields with fire. "Be silent, and know that I am God! I will be honored by every nation. I will be honored throughout the world."*

God's strength is revealed in his sovereign providence over all things. Nothing happens without God directing it or allowing it. He is in control of the entire universe.

Psalm 66:5 *Come and see what our God has done, what awesome miracles he does for his people!* God demonstrates his strength through the mighty miracles he has done for his people.

Acts 9:20-21 *Immediately [Saul] began preaching about Jesus in the synagogues, saying, "He is indeed the Son of God!" All who heard him were amazed. "Isn't this the same man who persecuted Jesus' followers . . . ?" they asked.* God transforms lives through the power of the gospel of Jesus Christ.

Revelation 18:8 *The sorrows of death and mourning and famine will overtake her in a single day. She will be utterly consumed by fire, for the Lord God who judges her is mighty.*

God has the strength and power to judge sin.

How can I experience the strength of God in my life?

Ephesians 1:19-23 *I pray that you will begin to understand the incredible greatness of his power for us who believe him.*

You already have his power in you—the power of the Resurrection—because you have trusted in Christ for salvation.

Isaiah 41:10 *Don't be afraid, for I am with you. Do not be dismayed, for I am your God. I will strengthen you. I will help you. I will uphold you with my victorious right hand.*

Acts 1:8 *But when the Holy Spirit has come upon you, you will receive power and will tell people about me everywhere—in Jerusalem, throughout Judea, in Samaria, and to the ends of the earth.*

You can experience God's power by trusting that he is with you.

Judges 6:15-16 *"But Lord," Gideon replied, "how can I rescue Israel? My clan is the weakest in the whole tribe of Manasseh, and I am the least in my entire family!" The LORD said to him, "I will be with you. And you will destroy the Midianites as if you were fighting against one man."*

Judges 7:4, 7 *But the LORD told Gideon, "There are still too many! Bring them down to the spring, and I will sort out who will go with you and who will not." . . . The Lord told Gideon, "With these three hundred men I will rescue you and give you victory over the Midianites."*

As strange as it sounds, you can experience his power in your weakness. When you recognize your weaknesses, and yet do great things for God, you know for certain that it is God's strength working through you.

How can I become stronger in my faith?

John 15:4-5 *Remain in me, and I will remain in you. For a branch cannot produce fruit if it is severed from the vine, and you cannot be fruitful apart from me. Yes, I am the vine; you are the branches. Those who remain in me, and I in them, will produce much fruit. For apart from me you can do nothing.*

Your faith is strengthened as you remain in constant fellowship with God through your relationship with Jesus Christ.

1 John 2:14 *I have written to you who are young because you are strong with God's word living in your hearts, and you have won your battle with Satan.*

Your faith is strengthened as you feed on God's Word.

Deuteronomy 11:8 *Be careful to obey every command I am giving you today, so you may have strength to go in and occupy the land you are about to enter.*

Your faith is strengthened when you live in obedience.

Jude 1:20 *Continue to build your lives on the foundation of your holy faith. And continue to pray as you are directed by the Holy Spirit.*
The Holy Spirit strengthens your faith through prayer.

2 Corinthians 12:10 *Since I know it is all for Christ's good, I am quite content with my weaknesses and with insults, hardships, persecutions, and calamities. For when I am weak, then I am strong.*
Your faith grows stronger through trials and troubles.

Romans 1:11 *I long to visit you so I can share a spiritual blessing with you that will help you grow strong in the Lord.*
Your faith grows stronger through the mutual encouragement and accountability of other believers.

How do I tap into God's strength to fight the battles of life?

Ephesians 6:10-16 *A final word: Be strong with the Lord's mighty power. Put on all of God's armor so that you will be able to stand firm against all strategies and tricks of the Devil. For we are not fighting against people made of flesh and blood, but against the evil rulers and authorities of the unseen world, against those mighty powers of darkness who*

227

rule this world, and against wicked spirits in the heavenly realms. Use every piece of God's armor to resist the enemy in the time of evil, so that after the battle you will still be standing firm. Stand your ground, putting on the sturdy belt of truth and the body armor of God's righteousness. For shoes, put on the peace that comes from the Good News, so that you will be fully prepared. In every battle you will need faith as your shield to stop the fiery arrows aimed at you by Satan.

Spiritual battles must be fought with spiritual weapons. Pray for God to arm you and equip you for battle.

Joshua 1:7-8 *Be strong and very courageous. Obey all the laws Moses gave you. Do not turn away from them, and you will be successful in everything you do. Study this Book of the Law continually. Meditate on it day and night so you may be sure to obey all that is written in it. Only then will you succeed.*

God's Word is your secret weapon in fighting the battles of life because in it you find the battle strategy as outlined by God Almighty himself. God, the Creator of life, tells how to live life to the fullest. But if you don't study God's Word, you will miss the strategies that will help you overcome anything life throws at you.

1 Timothy 6:12 *Fight the good fight for what we believe. Hold tightly to the eternal life that God*

has given you, which you have confessed so well before many witnesses.

2 Timothy 4:7 *I have fought a good fight, I have finished the race, and I have remained faithful.* Always keep your eyes on the end goal, which is heaven. In this life you will face struggles, hardships, and spiritual battles. But if you make each decision as if you are investing in eternity, your life will make sense and have purpose and direction.

1 Corinthians 1:8-9 *He will keep you strong right up to the end, and he will keep you free from all blame on the great day when our Lord Jesus Christ returns. God will surely do this for you, for he always does just what he says, and he is the one who invited you into this wonderful friendship with his Son, Jesus Christ our Lord.*

Philippians 4:13 *For I can do everything with the help of Christ who gives me the strength I need.* Don't underestimate the strength that God provides, if you just ask him. Claim God's promises, walk in his presence, embrace his protection, and you will be strong enough to face any foe.

PROMISE FROM GOD Psalm 28:7 *The LORD is my strength, my shield from every danger. I trust in him with all my heart. He helps me, and my heart is filled with joy. I burst out in songs of thanksgiving.*

Stress

(*see also* ADVERSITY)

How can I deal with stress?

Psalm 55:22 *Give your burdens to the LORD, and he will take care of you. He will not permit the godly to slip and fall.*

Matthew 11:28 *Come to me, all of you who are weary and carry heavy burdens, and I will give you rest.*
Recognize that God brings true peace of heart and mind. The first step in dealing with stress is to bring your burdens to the Lord.

2 Samuel 22:7 *But in my distress I cried out to the LORD. . . . He heard me from his sanctuary; my cry reached his ears.*
Be persistent in prayer.

2 Corinthians 4:9 *We are hunted down, but God never abandons us. We get knocked down, but we get up again and keep going.*
Be aware that problems and pressures are inevitable. But even in the midst of them, God is invincible.

Mark 6:31 *Then Jesus said, "Let's get away from the crowds for a while and rest." There were so many people coming and going that Jesus and his apostles didn't even have time to eat.*

Make time to slow down and take a break from pressure-packed situations.

1 Timothy 5:23 *Don't drink only water. You ought to drink a little wine for the sake of your stomach because you are sick so often.*
Take care of your body. Adequate rest, regular exercise, and proper nutrition are useful tools for dealing with stress.

Galatians 6:9 *Don't get tired of doing what is good. Don't get discouraged and give up, for we will reap a harvest of blessing at the appropriate time.*
Deal with stress. Don't let stress defeat you. When you are tired of doing good, it may be because you are just too tired.

Our true character is exposed when we are under stress. How do I respond to stress so that something good can come from it?
Romans 5:3 *We can rejoice, too, when we run into problems and trials, for we know that they are good for us—they help us learn to endure.*

James 1:2-4 *Dear brothers and sisters, whenever trouble comes your way, let it be an opportunity for joy. For when your faith is tested, your endurance has a chance to grow. So let it grow, for when your endurance is fully developed, you will be strong in character and ready for anything.*
Character is built from the positive building blocks of life. But it is also built from conquering

the stresses and problems of life. What you do with stress not only reveals your character but also helps develop your character.

PROMISE FROM GOD John 16:33
I have told you all this so that you may have peace in me. Here on earth you will have many trials and sorrows. But take heart, because I have overcome the world.

Suffering

Why do I experience suffering? Why does God let anyone suffer?

Genesis 37:28 *So when the traders came by, his brothers pulled Joseph out of the pit and sold him for twenty pieces of silver.*

Joshua 7:1 *A man named Achan had stolen some of these things, so the LORD was very angry with the Israelites.*

Sometimes you suffer because of the sins of others, not your own sins.

John 9:2-3 *"Teacher," his disciples asked him, "why was this man born blind? Was it a result of his own sins or those of his parents?" "It was not because of his sins or his parents' sins," Jesus answered.*

Sometimes the suffering that comes to you is not your fault. It just happens. In this case, how you react to the suffering is the key.

Proverbs 3:11-12 *My child, don't ignore it when the LORD disciplines you. . . . For the LORD corrects those he loves, just as a father corrects a child in whom he delights.*
Sometimes God sends suffering as a consequence for your sins. He disciplines you because he loves you and wants to correct you and restore you to him.

Deuteronomy 8:2 *Remember how the LORD your God led you through the wilderness for forty years, humbling you and testing you . . . to find out whether or not you would really obey his commands.*
Sometimes God tests you with suffering to encourage you to obey him.

1 Peter 4:14 *Be happy if you are insulted for being a Christian, for then the glorious Spirit of God will come upon you.*
Sometimes you suffer because you must take a stand for Christ.

James 1:3 *When your faith is tested, your endurance has a chance to grow.*
Sometimes you suffer because it will help you to grow and mature.

2 Timothy 3:12 *Yes, and everyone who wants to live a godly life in Christ Jesus will suffer persecution.*
The world hates Christ, so when you identify with him, you can expect the world that inflicted suffering on him to also inflict suffering on you.

Does God care when I am suffering?

Psalm 23:4 *Even when I walk through the dark valley of death, I will not be afraid, for you are close beside me. Your rod and your staff protect and comfort me.*

God sticks with you even in your most intense suffering.

Psalm 56:8 *You keep track of all my sorrows. You have collected all my tears in your bottle. You have recorded each one in your book.*

Your suffering matters to God because *you* matter to God.

John 11:33-35 *When Jesus saw her weeping and saw the other people wailing with her, he was moved with indignation and was deeply troubled. "Where have you put him?" he asked them. They told him, "Lord, come and see." Then Jesus wept.*

Isaiah 53:3 *He was despised and rejected—a man of sorrows, acquainted with the bitterest grief.*

Jesus hurts when you hurt. He not only cares, but he also shares your sorrows.

Can any good come from my suffering?

Job 5:17-18 *But consider the joy of those corrected by God! Do not despise the chastening of the Almighty when you sin. For though he wounds, he also bandages. He strikes, but his hands also heal.*

Suffering can bring great renewal and healing if it drives you to God.

Romans 5:3-4 *We can rejoice, too, when we run into problems and trials, for we know that they are good for us—they help us learn to endure. And endurance develops strength of character.*

2 Timothy 2:10 *I am willing to endure anything if it will bring salvation and eternal glory in Christ Jesus to those God has chosen.*
When suffering is for your good, Christ's glory, and the building of his church, you should be happy to accept it.

2 Corinthians 1:3-4 *All praise to the God and Father of our Lord Jesus Christ. He is the source of every mercy and the God who comforts us. He comforts us . . . so that we can comfort others.*
Suffering enables you to give comfort to others. Wounded healers are more welcome than healers who have never been wounded. Why? Because they know they don't have all they answers, and they have wrestled and agonized over the questions. Woundedness may appear to weaken you, but it actually better enables you to minister to the suffering.

How do I stay close to God in times of suffering?

Psalm 22:24 *For he has not ignored the suffering of the needy. He has not turned and walked away. He has listened to their cries for help.*

Recognize that God has not abandoned you in times of suffering.

Psalm 126:5-6 *Those who plant in tears will harvest with shouts of joy. They weep as they go to plant their seed, but they sing as they return with the harvest.*

Recognize that suffering is not forever. In the dark hours of the night of suffering it is hard to think of a morning of joy and gladness. But the tears of suffering are like seeds of joy.

Lamentations 3:32-33 *Though he brings grief, he also shows compassion according to the greatness of his unfailing love. For he does not enjoy hurting people or causing them sorrow.*

Recognize that a loving God does not enjoy seeing you suffer. But his compassionate love and care will see you through your times of discipline and suffering.

Matthew 17:12 *And soon the Son of Man will also suffer at their hands.*

Luke 24:26 *Wasn't it clearly predicted by the prophets that the Messiah would have to suffer all these things before entering his time of glory?*

Hebrews 2:18 *Since he himself has gone through suffering and temptation, he is able to help us when we are being tempted.*

Recognize that Jesus himself suffered for you. Christ suffered the agonies of the cross, which not only embraced incredible physical suffering but also the unthinkable suffering of bearing the sins of the world.

Romans 8:17-18 *Since we are his children, we will share his treasures—for everything God gives to his Son, Christ, is ours, too. But if we are to share his glory, we must also share his suffering. Yet what we suffer now is nothing compared to the glory he will give us later.*

Recognize that all suffering will end forever when those who believe in Jesus are welcomed into heaven.

How can I respond to the suffering of others?

1 Corinthians 12:26 *If one part suffers, all parts suffer with it, and if one part is honored, all the parts are glad.*

When one Christian suffers, it should hurt us all, for we are all members of Christ's body. If one part of our physical body hurts, it affects the entire body. So it should be in the body of Christ. If you know someone who is hurting, suffer along with that person.

Romans 12:15 *When others are happy, be happy with them. If they are sad, share their sorrow.*

Suffering people need empathy, not advice.

Galatians 6:2 *Share each other's troubles and problems, and in this way obey the law of Christ.*

Luke 10:34 *Kneeling beside him, the Samaritan soothed his wounds with medicine and bandaged them. Then he put the man on his own donkey and took him to an inn, where he took care of him.*
Seek to provide whatever practical support you can for a person who is suffering.

PROMISE FROM GOD Zechariah 9:12 *Come back to the place of safety . . . for there is yet hope! I promise this very day that I will repay you two mercies for each of your woes!*

$\mathcal{S}ympathy$

Does the Lord really sympathize with me in my time of need?
Psalm 103:13-14 *The LORD is like a father to his children, tender and compassionate to those who fear him. For he understands how weak we are; he knows we are only dust.*
There is no trouble that comes to you without the watchful eye of your heavenly Father seeing it and sympathizing with you. To know that he knows is the beginning of healing.

Matthew 9:36 *He felt great pity for the crowds that came, because their problems were so great and they didn't know where to go for help. They were like sheep without a shepherd.*

Hebrews 4:15 *This High Priest of ours under-stands our weaknesses, for he faced all of the same temptations we do, yet he did not sin.*
The story of Jesus is a story of tender compassion toward those in need. There is no temptation, hurt, or pain that comes into your life without touching the sympathetic heart of Jesus. Jesus knows and cares.

How can I show sympathy to others?

Hebrews 10:33 *Sometimes you were exposed to public ridicule and were beaten, and sometimes you helped others who were suffering the same things.*
By feeling deeply what the other person is going through.

Luke 10:36-37 *"Now which of these three would you say was a neighbor to the man who was attacked by bandits?" Jesus asked. The man replied, "The one who showed him mercy." Then Jesus said, "Yes, now go and do the same."*
By helping the person in need.

2 Corinthians 1:4 *When others are troubled, we will be able to give them the same comfort God has given us.*
By sharing words of encouragement.

PROMISE FROM GOD 1 Peter 3:8
Finally, all of you should be of one mind, full of sympathy toward each other, loving one another with tender hearts and humble minds.

Terrorism

(*see also* FEAR)

How can I avoid living in constant fear?

P s a l m   2 7 : 1   *The LORD is my light and my salvation—so why should I be afraid? The LORD protects me from danger—so why should I tremble?*
Trusting that God is in control of the world, that he is all-powerful, and that he will one day judge all people and punish the wicked can free you from crippling fear.

M a t t h e w   1 0 : 2 8   *Don't be afraid of those who want to kill you. They can only kill your body; they cannot touch your soul.*
Remembering that your eternity is secure in Christ and untouchable by terrorists can build your confidence.

M a t t h e w   6 : 3 4   *So don't worry about tomorrow, for tomorrow will bring its own worries. Today's trouble is enough for today.*
Refuse to panic about what might happen. Fretting about the unknowable future is only debilitating. The "what if" worries are a waste of time.

Does living by faith mean I should not take precautions?

A c t s   9 : 2 9 - 3 0   *He debated with some Greek-speaking Jews, but they plotted to murder him. When the believers heard about it, however, they took him to Caesarea and sent him on to his hometown of Tarsus.*

Faith is different from foolhardiness. God often gives us the wisdom to take precautions. Take such actions not because you are overcome by terror but because you are acting wisely.

How should I pray in this time of terrorism?

P s a l m   7 : 6 *Arise, O LORD, in anger! Stand up against the fury of my enemies! Wake up, my God, and bring justice!*

It is appropriate to be outraged by acts of terrorism and to pray that God will protect you and bring terrorists to justice.

M a t t h e w   5 : 4 3 - 4 4 *You have heard that the law of Moses says, "Love your neighbor" and hate your enemy. But I say, love your enemies! Pray for those who persecute you.*

You can pray that terrorists will find God's love and that their lives will be transformed. This is not contradictory to the prayer that God will judge terrorists since both mercy and justice are part of God's character.

M a t t h e w   6 : 1 0 *May your Kingdom come soon. May your will be done here on earth, just as it is in heaven.*

It is important to pray not just against terrorism

but for God's purposes and to look forward to the fulfillment of God's Kingdom at the return of Jesus.

PROMISE FROM GOD Isaiah 41:10 *Don't be afraid, for I am with you. Do not be dismayed, for I am your God. I will strengthen you. I will help you. I will uphold you with my victorious right hand.*

Thankfulness

What can I be thankful for?

Mark 6:41 *Jesus took the five loaves and two fish, looked up toward heaven, and asked God's blessing on the food.*
You can thank God for his provision of life's basic needs, such as food, clothing, shelter, and life itself.

Psalm 13:5-6 *But I trust in your unfailing love. I will rejoice because you have rescued me. I will sing to the LORD because he has been so good to me.*
You can thank God for helping you through your troubles.

Psalm 44:7 *It is you who gives us victory over our enemies.*
You can thank God when you have experienced success.

1 Samuel 18:3 *And Jonathan made a special vow to be David's friend.*
You can thank God for friendships.

James 1:17 *Whatever is good and perfect comes to us from God above, who created all heaven's lights. Unlike them, he never changes or casts shifting shadows.*
You can thank God for everything good in your world and in your life.

Are there things I can be thankful for even when circumstances are not going well?

1 Chronicles 16:34 *Give thanks to the LORD, for he is good! His faithful love endures forever.*

1 Corinthians 15:57 *How we thank God, who gives us victory over sin and death through Jesus Christ our Lord!*

2 Corinthians 9:15 *Thank God for his Son— a gift too wonderful for words!*

1 Thessalonians 5:18 *No matter what happens, always be thankful, for this is God's will for you who belong to Christ Jesus.*
You can thank the Lord for being good and just. You can thank him for his unchanging, perfect character. You can thank him also for his love for you, his faithfulness, for sending his Son Jesus, for his mercy. You can thank him for victory over death and for keeping his promises.

How can I develop an attitude of thanksgiving?

Psalm 136:24-26 *He saved us from our enemies. His faithful love endures forever. He gives food to every living thing. His faithful love endures forever. Give thanks to the God of heaven. His faithful love endures forever.*

Discipline yourself to make some time every day for thanksgiving. Make a mental list of God's blessings in your life—especially the most recent ones—and thank him for them. Don't wait to feel thankful before giving thanks. Giving thanks will lead you to feel thankful.

PROMISE FROM GOD Psalm 147:1 *Praise the LORD! How good it is to sing praises to our God! How delightful and how right!*

Timing of God

How can I be patient as I wait for God's timing?

Psalm 59:9 *You are my strength; I wait for you to rescue me, for you, O God, are my place of safety.*
Remind yourself continually of God's faithfulness. He is actively working in your life to help you become all he made you to be.

Romans 12:12 *Be glad for all God is planning*

for you. Be patient in trouble, and always be
prayerful.
Be steadfast in prayer.

PROMISE FROM GOD Habakkuk
2:3 *These things I plan won't happen right away.*
Slowly, steadily, surely, the time approaches when the
vision will be fulfilled. If it seems slow, wait patiently,
for it will surely take place. It will not be delayed.

Tragedy

(*see also* ADVERSITY or GRIEF or SUFFERING)

What causes tragedy? Does God send or allow tragedy?

Daniel 9:14 *The LORD has brought against us*
the disaster he prepared, for we did not obey him,
and the LORD our God is just in everything he does.

Jeremiah 44:23 *The very reason all these terri-*
ble things have happened to you is because you have
burned incense to idols and sinned against the LORD,
refusing to obey him and follow his instructions, laws,
and stipulations.

Tragedy sometimes occurs because of sin—our
own sin or others' sins.

Deuteronomy 30:15-16, 19-20 *Now*
listen! Today I am giving you a choice between
prosperity and disaster, between life and death. I have

commanded you today to love the LORD your God and to keep his commands, laws, and regulations by walking in his ways. . . . Oh, that you would choose life, that you and your descendants might live! Choose to love the LORD your God and to obey him and commit yourself to him, for he is your life. Then you will live long in the land the LORD swore to give your ancestors Abraham, Isaac, and Jacob.

Tragedy is sometimes caused by ignoring God's wisdom. The rules and laws he gives are not meant to squelch pleasure or fun; instead, they are the way to life and health for us.

M i c a h 3 : 1 - 5 *Listen, you leaders of Israel! You are supposed to know right from wrong, but you are the very ones who hate good and love evil. You skin my people alive and tear the flesh off their bones. You eat my people's flesh, cut away their skin, and break their bones. You chop them up like meat for the cooking pot. Then you beg the LORD for help in times of trouble! Do you really expect him to listen? After all the evil you have done, he won't even look at you! This is what the LORD says to you false prophets: "You are leading my people astray! You promise peace for those who give you food, but you declare war on anyone who refuses to pay you."*

Tragedy is sometimes caused by ungodly leadership.

I s a i a h 4 5 : 7 *I am the one who creates the light and makes the darkness. I am the one who sends good times and bad times. I, the* LORD, *am the one who does these things.*

John 9:1-3 *As Jesus was walking along, he saw a man who had been blind from birth. "Teacher," his disciples asked him, "why was this man born blind? Was it a result of his own sins or those of his parents?" "It was not because of his sins or his parents' sins," Jesus answered. "He was born blind so the power of God could be seen in him."*

Luke 13:1-5 *About this time Jesus was informed that Pilate had murdered some people from Galilee as they were sacrificing at the Temple in Jerusalem. "Do you think those Galileans were worse sinners than other people from Galilee?" he asked. "Is that why they suffered? Not at all! And you will also perish unless you turn from your evil ways and turn to God. And what about the eighteen men who died when the Tower of Siloam fell on them? Were they the worst sinners in Jerusalem? No, and I tell you again that unless you repent, you will also perish."* God does both cause and allow tragedy—often tied to sin, but sometimes unrelated to any sin. While we may not always understand the *why* behind life's tragic circumstances, we can trust that God remains both sovereign and loving.

How does God help in times of tragedy?

Psalm 10:17 LORD, *you know the hopes of the help-less. Surely you will listen to their cries and comfort them.*

Psalm 55:17 *Morning, noon, and night I plead aloud in my distress, and the LORD hears my voice.* God listens to your prayers.

Psalm 118:5 *In my distress I prayed to the LORD, and the LORD answered me and rescued me.*

Nehemiah 9:27 *So you handed them over to their enemies. But in their time of trouble they cried to you, and you heard them from heaven. In great mercy, you sent them deliverers who rescued them from their enemies.* God responds to your calls for help.

Psalm 91:9-16 *If you make the LORD your refuge, if you make the Most High your shelter, no evil will conquer you; no plague will come near your dwelling. For he orders his angels to protect you wherever you go. They will hold you with their hands to keep you from striking your foot on a stone. You will trample down lions and poisonous snakes; you will crush fierce lions and serpents under your feet! The LORD says, "I will rescue those who love me. I will protect those who trust in my name. When they call on me, I will answer; I will be with them in trouble. I will rescue them and honor them. I will satisfy them with a long life and give them my salvation."* God shows himself, making his presence and his character known.

Psalm 130:5 *I am counting on the LORD; yes, I am counting on him. I have put my hope in his word.* God comforts and guides with his Word.

Psalm 119:76 *Now let your unfailing love comfort me, just as you promised me, your servant.*

Psalm 33:22 *Let your unfailing love surround us, LORD, for our hope is in you alone.*

Most importantly, God continues to love you.

How should I handle tragedy?

Romans 8:34-37 *Who then will condemn us? Will Christ Jesus? No, for he is the one who died for us and was raised to life for us and is sitting at the place of highest honor next to God, pleading for us. Can anything ever separate us from Christ's love? Does it mean he no longer loves us if we have trouble or calamity, or are persecuted, or are hungry or cold or in danger or threatened with death? (Even the Scriptures say, "For your sake we are killed every day; we are being slaughtered like sheep.") No, despite all these things, overwhelming victory is ours through Christ, who loved us.*

Whatever the cause, whatever the circumstances, face life in full assurance of God's unfailing love for you.

Proverbs 10:25 *Disaster strikes like a cyclone, whirling the wicked away, but the godly have a lasting foundation.*

Matthew 7:24-27 *Anyone who listens to my teaching and obeys me is wise, like a person who builds a house on solid rock. Though the rain comes in torrents and the floodwaters rise and the winds beat against that house, it won't collapse, because it is built on rock. But anyone who hears my teaching and ignores it is foolish, like a person who builds a house on sand. When the rains and floods come and the winds beat against that house, it will fall with a mighty crash.*

While tragedy is most often sudden and unexpected, your daily relationship with God prepares you for times of trouble. You may not be able to understand what is happening, but you can place your trust in something solid and secure—God and his faithfulness.

Psalm 77:1 *I cry out to God without holding back. Oh, that God would listen to me!*

Psalm 120:1 *I took my troubles to the LORD; I cried out to him, and he answered my prayer.*

Jeremiah 17:17 *LORD, do not desert me now! You alone are my hope in the day of disaster.*
Go directly and immediately to God to trust him, to listen to him, and to obey him.

2 Corinthians 6:4 *In everything we do we try to show that we are true ministers of God. We patiently endure troubles and hardships and calamities of every kind.*
Patiently endure. Tragedy is not new, but that doesn't make it any less surprising or any less painful. Ask God to give you the strength to endure so that your life glorifies him.

Psalm 50:15 *Trust me in your times of trouble, and I will rescue you, and you will give me glory.* Trust God, and then readily give him the credit for all he does to care for you.

How can I help others cope with tragedy?

Psalm 20:1 *In times of trouble, may the LORD respond to your cry. May the God of Israel keep you safe from all harm.*

1 Kings 17:20 *Then Elijah cried out to the LORD, "O LORD my God, why have you brought tragedy on this widow who has opened her home to me, causing her son to die?"* You can intercede in prayer for them.

Nehemiah 2:17 *I said to them, "You know full well the tragedy of our city. It lies in ruins, and its gates are burned. Let us rebuild the wall of Jerusalem and rid ourselves of this disgrace!"* You can encourage them to follow God.

Romans 15:26 *The believers in Greece have eagerly taken up an offering for the Christians in Jerusalem, who are going through such hard times.* You can meet their physical needs in practical, compassionate ways.

PROMISE FROM GOD: Jeremiah 29:11 *"For I know the plans I have for you," says the LORD. "They are plans for good and not for disaster, to give you a future and a hope."*

Troubled Times

How should I respond when trouble comes?

Isaiah 37:14-20 *After Hezekiah received the letter and read it, he went up to the LORD's Temple and spread it out before the LORD. And Hezekiah prayed this prayer before the LORD: "O LORD Almighty, God of Israel, you are enthroned between the mighty cherubim! You alone are God of all the kingdoms of the earth. You alone created the heavens and the earth. Listen to me, O LORD, and hear! Open your eyes, O LORD, and see! Listen to Sennacherib's words of defiance against the living God.*

"It is true, LORD, that the kings of Assyria have destroyed all these nations, just as the message says. And they have thrown the gods of these nations into the fire and burned them. But of course the Assyrians could destroy them! They were not gods at all—only idols of wood and stone shaped by human hands. Now, O LORD our God, rescue us from his power; then all the kingdoms of the earth will know that you alone, O LORD, are God."

Psalm 142:2 *I pour out my complaints before him and tell him all my troubles.*

Immediately go to God—in honesty and in faith. King Hezekiah faced what looked like a hopeless situation. So he took the threatening letter right to God's temple and spread it out before the Lord, crying out for God's rescue. Whatever situation is troubling you, take it directly to God's throne, lay it out, and ask God to give you help, wisdom, and guidance.

Psalm 25:16-18 *Turn to me and have mercy on me, for I am alone and in deep distress. My problems go from bad to worse. Oh, save me from them all! Feel my pain and see my trouble. Forgive all my sins.* Check your heart. God sometimes uses the consequences of sin to draw us back to repentance, not to get even with us. When trouble strikes, you need to search your heart to see if the problem might be a result of your own wrongdoing. If it is, you need to ask God's help in dealing with it. If it isn't, you still have the benefit of drawing closer to God.

Psalm 119:143 *As pressure and stress bear down on me, I find joy in your commands.*

Matthew 13:21 *But like young plants in such soil, their roots don't go very deep. At first they get along fine, but they wilt as soon as they have problems or are persecuted because they believe the word.* Delve into God's Word. God has given us his Word as a source of comfort, joy, guidance, and nourishment. If you want to hear him speak to you, you need to open the book and read.

Matthew 6:34 *Don't worry about tomorrow, for tomorrow will bring its own worries. Today's trouble is enough for today.*

Don't be overcome by worry. Borrowing troubles from tomorrow through worry can cause physical, spiritual, and emotional bankruptcy.

Ecclesiastes 8:6 *Yes, there is a time and a way for everything, even as people's troubles lie heavily upon them.*
Be open to options and look for God's creative solution.

Jeremiah 42:13-17 *But if you refuse to obey the LORD your God and say, "We will not stay here," and if you insist on going to live in Egypt where you think you will be free from war, famine, and alarms, then this is what the LORD says to the remnant of Judah. The LORD Almighty, the God of Israel, says: "If you insist on going to Egypt, the war and famine you fear will follow close behind you, and you will die there. That is the fate awaiting every one of you who insists on going to live in Egypt. Yes, you will die from war, famine, and disease. None of you will escape from the disaster I will bring upon you there."*
Be obedient to what you know of God's will—even if you don't know exactly what to do in this particular situation. Jeremiah begged his people to be obedient and trust in God, but they refused. Sometimes we think running away from trouble will make it go away—but some kinds of trouble will follow us wherever we go. Sometimes we need to stay and work through it. So seek God's guidance as you work through the difficult situation.

Galatians 6:2 *Share each other's troubles and problems, and in this way obey the law of Christ.* Gain strength and support from other Christians.

Daniel 3:16-18 *Shadrach, Meshach, and Abednego replied, "O Nebuchadnezzar, we do not need to defend ourselves before you. If we are thrown into the blazing furnace, the God whom we serve is able to save us. He will rescue us from your power, Your Majesty. But even if he doesn't, Your Majesty can be sure that we will never serve your gods or worship the gold statue you have set up."* Be fully committed to God and trust him with the outcome.

2 Corinthians 1:3-5 *All praise to the God and Father of our Lord Jesus Christ. He is the source of every mercy and the God who comforts us. He comforts us in all our troubles so that we can comfort others. When others are troubled, we will be able to give them the same comfort God has given us. You can be sure that the more we suffer for Christ, the more God will shower us with his comfort through Christ.* Be ever confident and full of praise to God—even when you don't feel like it. Patiently and prayerfully look upward to God in praise and gladness.

How does God help me in my times of trouble?

Matthew 8:23-27 *Then Jesus got into the boat and started across the lake with his disciples.*

Suddenly, a terrible storm came up, with waves breaking into the boat. But Jesus was sleeping. The disciples went to him and woke him up, shouting, "Lord, save us! We're going to drown!" And Jesus answered, "Why are you afraid? You have so little faith!" Then he stood up and rebuked the wind and waves, and suddenly all was calm. The disciples just sat there in awe. "Who is this?" they asked themselves. "Even the wind and waves obey him!"

Psalm 25:17 *My problems go from bad to worse. Oh, save me from them all!*
God is bigger than any trouble you may face. Nothing surprises him, scares him, or intimidates him.

Psalm 22:11 *Do not stay so far from me, for trouble is near, and no one else can help me.*
God knows all about your trouble and is ready and able to help you.

Psalm 31:7,9 *I am overcome with joy because of your unfailing love, for you have seen my troubles, and you care about the anguish of my soul. . . . Have mercy on me, LORD, for I am in distress. My sight is blurred because of my tears. My body and soul are withering away.*

Psalm 9:9, 12 *The LORD is a shelter for the oppressed, a refuge in times of trouble. . . . For he who avenges murder cares for the helpless. He does not ignore those who cry to him for help.*
God is loving, caring, merciful, and attentive.

Psalm 18:6 *In my distress I cried out to the LORD; yes, I prayed to my God for help. He heard me from his sanctuary; my cry reached his ears.*

Psalm 34:17 *The LORD hears his people when they call to him for help. He rescues them from all their troubles.*

God hears and answers your prayers.

Isaiah 43:2 *When you go through deep waters and great trouble, I will be with you. When you go through rivers of difficulty, you will not drown! When you walk through the fire of oppression, you will not be burned up; the flames will not consume you.*

Jonah 2:2 *He said, "I cried out to the LORD in my great trouble, and he answered me. I called to you from the world of the dead, and LORD, you heard me!"*

God is with you in times of trouble.

John 14:27 *I am leaving you with a gift—peace of mind and heart. And the peace I give isn't like the peace the world gives. So don't be troubled or afraid.*

1 Peter 5:7 *Give all your worries and cares to God, for he cares about what happens to you.*

God offers to replace your fear with his peace.

Psalm 34:19 *The righteous face many troubles, but the LORD rescues them from each and every one.*

Psalm 50:15 *Trust me in your times of trouble, and I will rescue you, and you will give me glory.*

God promises he will rescue and save you because he loves you.

What can I learn from my troubles? What good can come from times of trouble?

Romans 8:28 *And we know that God causes everything to work together for the good of those who love God and are called according to his purpose for them.*

Psalm 107:43 *Those who are wise will take all this to heart; they will see in our history the faithful love of the LORD.*

God is always working in your life. Although you may not see his plan or even his activity in the midst of trouble, you can trust his love for you. Look back through your own history and remember how God has faithfully shown his love to you, especially through times of trouble.

2 Corinthians 6:3-7 *We try to live in such a way that no one will be hindered from finding the Lord by the way we act, and so no one can find fault with our ministry. In everything we do we try to show that we are true ministers of God. We patiently endure troubles and hardships and calamities of every kind. We have been beaten, been put in jail, faced angry mobs, worked to exhaustion, endured sleepless nights, and gone without food. We have proved ourselves by our purity, our understanding, our patience, our kindness, our sincere love, and the power of the Holy Spirit. We have faithfully preached the truth. God's power has been working in us. We have righteousness as our weapon, both to attack and to defend ourselves.*

God's power works within the lives of those who follow him.

Philippians 1:12-14 *And I want you to know, dear brothers and sisters, that everything that has happened to me here has helped to spread the Good News. For everyone here, including all the soldiers in the palace guard, knows that I am in chains because of Christ. And because of my imprisonment, many of the Christians here have gained confidence and become more bold in telling others about Christ.*

Acts 8:3-4 *Saul was going everywhere to devastate the church. He went from house to house, dragging out both men and women to throw them into jail. But the believers who had fled Jerusalem went everywhere preaching the Good News about Jesus.*

God can use your difficult circumstances for his kingdom's growth and for the good of others.

1 Peter 1:6-7 *So be truly glad! There is wonderful joy ahead, even though it is necessary for you to endure many trials for a while. These trials are only to test your faith, to show that it is strong and pure. It is being tested as fire tests and purifies gold—and your faith is far more precious to God than mere gold. So if your faith remains strong after being tried by fiery trials, it will bring you much praise and glory and honor on the day when Jesus Christ is revealed to the whole world.*

Proverbs 24:10 *If you fail under pressure, your strength is not very great.*
Troubles can test your faith, proving it pure and strong.

Deuteronomy 8:2-3 *Remember how the LORD your God led you through the wilderness for forty years, humbling you and testing you to prove your character, and to find out whether or not you would really obey his commands. Yes, he humbled you by letting you go hungry and then feeding you with manna, a food previously unknown to you and your ancestors. He did it to teach you that people need more than bread for their life; real life comes by feeding on every word of the LORD.*
Troubles can prove your character through lessons of obedience.

2 Corinthians 1:8-10 *I think you ought to know, dear brothers and sisters, about the trouble we went through in the province of Asia. We were crushed and completely overwhelmed, and we thought we would never live through it. In fact, we expected to die. But as a result, we learned not to rely on ourselves, but on God who can raise the dead. And he did deliver us from mortal danger. And we are confident that he will continue to deliver us.*
Troubles can help you learn to rely on God.

2 Corinthians 1:3-4, 6 *All praise to the God and Father of our Lord Jesus Christ. He is the source of every mercy and the God who comforts us. He*

*comforts us in all our troubles so that we can comfort
others. When others are troubled, we will be able to
give them the same comfort God has given us. . . .
So when we are weighed down with troubles, it is for
your benefit and salvation! For when God comforts
us, it is so that we, in turn, can be an encouragement
to you. Then you can patiently endure the same things
we suffer.*

Times of trouble can prepare you to minister
comfort to others in their times of trouble.

PROMISE FROM GOD Nahum 1:7
*The LORD is good. When trouble comes, he is a strong
refuge. And he knows everyone who trusts in him.*

Trust

(*see also* ASSURANCE and FAITH)

Why should I put my trust in God? How do I know he is trustworthy?

Numbers 23:19 *God is not a man, that he
should lie.*

Titus 1:2 *This truth gives them the confidence
of eternal life, which God promised before the world
began—and he cannot lie.*

You can trust God because he always tells the
truth.

Lamentations 3:22 *The unfailing love of the LORD never ends!*

Romans 5:8 *God showed his great love for us by sending Christ to die for us while we were still sinners.* You can trust God because God loves you and therefore always has your best interests at heart. The supreme guarantee of God's love is the sacrifice of his Son for you so that you might live forever with him in heaven.

Malachi 3:6 *I am the LORD, and I do not change.* You can trust God because he is eternally unchanging. You never have to worry whether his character or attitude toward you will be different tomorrow.

What does it mean to trust God? What should it look like in my life?

Psalm 33:21 *In him our hearts rejoice, for we are trusting in his holy name.* Trusting God means that you recognize that he is trustworthy and then, every day, in every situation, trust him above all else.

Genesis 6:14, 17, 22 *"Make a boat. . . . I am about to cover the earth with a flood." . . . Noah did everything exactly as God had commanded him.* Trusting God means that you obey his commands even when you don't fully understand.

John 3:36 *All who believe in God's Son have eternal life.*

Trusting God means that you depend on Christ alone for salvation.

Galatians 2:16 *No one will ever be saved by obeying the law.*
Trusting Christ for salvation means that you cease to trust in your own efforts to be righteous.

1 Peter 1:8 *Though you do not see him, you trust him.*
Trusting God means that you are confident in him even though you can't see him.

Why should I trust God?

1 John 4:16 *We know how much God loves us, and we have put our trust in him. God is love, and all who live in love live in God, and God lives in them.*

Psalm 9:10 *Those who know your name trust in you, for you, O LORD, have never abandoned anyone who searches for you.*

Psalm 147:11 *The LORD's delight is in those who honor him, those who put their hope in his unfailing love.*
God's character is trustworthy.

Hebrews 1:10-12 *Lord, in the beginning you laid the foundation of the earth, and the heavens are the work of your hands. Even they will perish, but you remain forever. They will wear out like old clothing. You will roll them up like an old coat. They will fade away like old clothing. But you are always the same; you will never grow old.*

Hebrews 13:8 *Jesus Christ is the same yesterday, today, and forever.*
God is unchanging and reliable.

Psalm 19:7 *The law of the LORD is perfect, reviving the soul. The decrees of the LORD are trustworthy, making wise the simple.*

Proverbs 30:5 *Every word of God proves true. He defends all who come to him for protection.*
God's Word is absolute truth.

Hebrews 6:18-19 *So God has given us both his promise and his oath. These two things are unchangeable because it is impossible for God to lie. Therefore, we who have fled to him for refuge can take new courage, for we can hold on to his promise with confidence. This confidence is like a strong and trustworthy anchor for our souls. It leads us through the curtain of heaven into God's inner sanctuary.*
God cannot lie.

2 Samuel 22:31 *As for God, his way is perfect. All the LORD's promises prove true. He is a shield for all who look to him for protection.*

2 Chronicles 6:14-15 *He prayed, "O LORD, God of Israel, there is no God like you in all of heaven and earth. You keep your promises and show unfailing love to all who obey you and are eager to do your will. You have kept your promise to your servant David, my father. You made that promise with your own mouth, and today you have fulfilled it with your own hands."*

Hebrews 10:23 *Without wavering, let us hold tightly to the hope we say we have, for God can be trusted to keep his promise.*

God always keeps his promises.

Psalm 18:30 *As for God, his way is perfect. All the LORD's promises prove true. He is a shield for all who look to him for protection.*

While it is good and necessary to trust others, God is the only one in whom you can completely trust. You can have complete assurance that what he says is true and what he does is reliable. That's because people, who are not prefect, will sometimes fail you, but God, who is perfect, will never fail you.

1 Peter 1:21 *Through Christ you have come to trust in God. And because God raised Christ from the dead and gave him great glory, your faith and hope can be placed confidently in God.*

John 12:44 *Jesus shouted to the crowds, "If you trust me, you are really trusting God who sent me."*

2 Corinthians 1:20 *All of God's promises have been fulfilled in him. That is why we say "Amen" when we give glory to God through Christ.*

Jesus' life, death, and resurrection lead you to trust God. All of God's promises have been fulfilled in Christ. Because all of those promises came true, you can trust that all of the rest of God's promises will also come true.

Exodus 14:31 *When the people of Israel saw the mighty power that the LORD had displayed against the Egyptians, they feared the LORD and put their faith in him and his servant Moses.*

2 Timothy 1:12 *I am suffering here in prison. But I am not ashamed of it, for I know the one in whom I trust, and I am sure that he is able to guard what I have entrusted to him until the day of his return.* God's power and strength have been demonstrated in your own life and in the lives of those around you. The undeniable facts of changed lives should give you confidence that you can trust who God is and what he can do.

PROMISE FROM GOD Isaiah 26:3 *You will keep in perfect peace all who trust in you, whose thoughts are fixed on you!*

War

(*see also* PEACE)

What does God think of war?

Genesis 1:27 *So God created people in his own image; God patterned them after himself; male and female he created them.*

Psalm 116:15 *The LORD's loved ones are precious to him; it grieves him when they die.*

Be careful about glorifying war and reveling in death—even the death of our enemies. God created every person and God loves every person. Therefore, anything that takes human life grieves God. So even if we conclude there are times when war is permissible or necessary, remember that war should always be our last resort.

Will God ever do anything about war?

Micah 4:3 *The LORD will settle international disputes. All the nations will beat their swords into plowshares and their spears into pruning hooks. All wars will stop, and military training will come to an end.*

Psalm 46:8-9 *Come, see the glorious works of the LORD: See how he brings destruction upon the world and causes wars to end throughout the earth. He breaks the bow and snaps the spear in two; he burns the shields with fire.*

When Jesus returns, war will be abolished forever. This is a cause for comfort and joy.

PROMISE FROM GOD Matthew 5:9 *God blesses those who work for peace, for they will be called the children of God*

Wisdom

How will having wisdom help me?

Ecclesiastes 10:10 *Since a dull ax requires*

great strength, sharpen the blade. That's the value of wisdom; it helps you succeed.
Wisdom will help you to succeed in what you do.

Ephesians 5:15 *Be careful how you live, not as fools but as those who are wise.*
Wisdom shows you how to live.

1 Kings 3:9 *Give me an understanding mind so that I can govern your people well and know the difference between right and wrong.*
The more responsibility you have, the more of God's wisdom you need in order to do what is right.

Proverbs 3:21-26 *My child, don't lose sight of good planning and insight. Hang on to them, for they fill you with life and bring you honor and respect. They keep you safe on your way and keep your feet from stumbling. You can lie down without fear and enjoy pleasant dreams. You need not be afraid of disaster or the destruction that comes upon the wicked, for the LORD is your security. He will keep your foot from being caught in a trap.*
Wisdom will preserve you from trouble and disaster.

Proverbs 9:11-12 *Wisdom will multiply your days and add years to your life. If you become wise, you will be the one to benefit. If you scorn wisdom, you will be the one to suffer.*
Wisdom will give you a more fulfilling life.

1 C o r i n t h i a n s 1 : 1 9 *I will destroy human wisdom and discard their most brilliant ideas.* Spiritual wisdom allows you to know the difference between what the Bible says is wise and what the world claims to be wise.

P r o v e r b s 5 : 1 - 2 *Pay attention to my wisdom. . . . Then you will learn to be discreet.* Wisdom protects you from evil.

How do I obtain wisdom?

J a m e s 1 : 5 *If you need wisdom . . . ask him, and he will gladly tell you. He will not resent your asking.* God promises to give wisdom to anyone who asks.

J o b 2 8 : 2 8 *The fear of the Lord is true wisdom; to forsake evil is real understanding.*

P r o v e r b s 9 : 1 0 *Fear of the LORD is the beginning of wisdom. Knowledge of the Holy One results in understanding.* Giving God first place in your life is a prerequisite for God's guidance. Asking God for wisdom is a hollow request if you are not willing to let God rule in your heart. Wisdom comes from having a relationship with God.

D e u t e r o n o m y 4 : 5 - 6 *You must obey these laws and regulations. . . . If you obey them carefully, you will display your wisdom and intelligence to the surrounding nations. When they hear about these*

laws, they will exclaim, "What other nation is as wise and prudent as this!"
Obedience to God's word—his commands, laws, and teachings—will make you wise.

1 John 2:27 *But you have received the Holy Spirit, and he lives within you, so you don't need anyone to teach you what is true. For the Spirit teaches you all things, and what he teaches is true—it is not a lie. So continue in what he has taught you, and continue to live in Christ.*
You find wisdom in the context of a relationship with God. When you are willing to be the learner, the Holy Spirit is willing to be your Teacher.

Proverbs 8:12, 17 *I, Wisdom, live together with good judgment. I know where to discover knowledge and discernment. . . . I love all who love me. Those who search for me will surely find me.*
You find wisdom when you seek it single-mindedly and wholeheartedly. Like many of the best things in life, to find wisdom you must pursue it.

Proverbs 20:18 *Plans succeed through good counsel; don't go to war without the advice of others.*
Wisdom often comes to you through the counsel of thoughtful, godly people.

Psalm 119:98 *Your commands make me wiser than my enemies, for your commands are my constant guide.*
God's Word is an unending source of wisdom for those who apply themselves to study it.

PROMISE FROM GOD Proverbs 1:23 *Come here and listen to me! I'll pour out the spirit of wisdom upon you and make you wise.*

Worry

When does worry become sin?

Matthew 13:22 *The thorny ground represents those who hear and accept the Good News, but all too quickly the message is crowded out by the cares of this life.*

Colossians 3:2 *Let heaven fill your thoughts. Do not think only about things down here on earth.* Worry over the concerns of life becomes sin when it prevents the Word of God from taking root in your life.

Why do I worry so much? How can I worry less?

Psalm 55:4 *My heart is in anguish. The terror of death overpowers me.*
Fear and anxiety are normal responses to threatening situations.

Exodus 14:13 *Moses told the people, "Don't be afraid. Just stand where you are and watch the LORD rescue you."*
You can combat worry and anxiety by remembering and trusting God's promises.

Philippians 4:6 *Don't worry about anything;*
instead, pray about everything.
You can combat worry by placing your cares
in Jesus' hands.

Psalm 62:6 *He alone is my rock and my salva-*
tion, my fortress where I will not be shaken.
You can find relief from fear in the promise
of salvation.

Matthew 6:27 *Can all your worries add a single*
moment to your life?
Your worries lose their grip on you as you focus
on kingdom priorities.

PROMISE FROM GOD 1 Peter 5:7
Give all your worries and cares to God, for he cares
about what happens to you.

Index

Alphabetical listing of all topics

If you enjoyed *TouchPoints for Troubled Times,* you will love the *TouchPoint Bible.*

The *TouchPoint Bible* is the most helpful Bible available for finding just the right Bible verses to meet an immediate need in your life or in the life of someone you are trying to help. With the exclusive HelpFinder Index, you have instant access to hundreds of key topics and thousands of Bible verses. The *TouchPoint Bible* also includes book introductions and Bible promises as well as hundreds of in-text application notes to help you apply God's truth to everyday life. Make the *TouchPoint Bible* your favorite Bible for church, devotional reading, or study.